This book is dedicated with love and gratitude to everyone throughout my life who have thought of me as Family. Your love and support have given me life and a will to keep loving! It has meant everything to me.

Kelli,

Thank you for being here to celebrate with me,

[signature]

SWERVE

The Tale of an Orphan Boy

INDEX

Chapter 1 – 442 Colonial Court

Chapter 2 – Clinton Gables

Chapter 3 – Hall of the Divine Child

Chapter 4 – The Cabin Up North

Chapter 5 – Anchor Bay Drive

Chapter 6 – The House in Mt. Clemens

Chapter 7 – Macomb County Youth Home

Chapter 8 – Mrs. Rae's Children's Home

Chapter 9 – The Macklems

Chapter 10 – The Schmidts

Chapter 11 – The Upper Room

Chapter 12 – The Day From Hell

Chapter 13 – St. Francis Infirmary

Chapter 14 – St. Francis Academy

Chapter 15 – Mr. Longo & ROTC

Chapter 16 – A Good Catholic Boy

Chapter 17 – BoysTown Freshman Year

Chapter 18 – BoysTown Sophomore Year

Chapter 19 – BoysTown Junior Year

Chapter 20 – BoysTown Senior Year

Chapter 21 – Coming Home

CHAPTER 1

442 Colonial Court

I'm about to tell you a story, but before I do so, it's important to begin by saying that long term memory is a tricky and unreliable thing. Any psychological professional can attest to that. A few pieces of this story were told to me by people I trust; people like my brother, Mike, and my cousin, Kathy. Some parts may seem a bit akimbo because my memory is no more reliable than anyone else's. Other parts may seem like they lack continuity and for that I beg your pardon. That said, this story is true. It may, or may not, necessarily be what actually happened, but it *is* true to the best of my recollection. To that recollection, flawed as it may be, I promise to be faithful. Let's begin:

***

Picture it: Detroit Michigan 1954. The American Auto industry is booming and the population of Detroit is cresting at just over one million people. Perry Como and Rosemary Clooney are on the top of the pop charts, Dwight Eisenhower is President of The United States, the average annual family household income in the US is $4,200. Senator Joseph McCarthy is convening his communist witch-hunt hearings in the Senate. Oh, and Benjamin Lester & Betty Jane Schroeder (nee Hutchenreuther) are at Catholic Social Services adopting a 2 year old orphan that they will come to name, Gregory Louis Schroeder.

That would be me! I am taken, by the couple, to my new home at 442 Colonial Court in Harper Woods to begin my new life. There,

I already have a 4-year-old brother named Michael Benjamin Schroeder, who is also adopted, and a beautiful Cocker Spaniel named Copper.

Les' Brother William Benjamin Schroeder, along with his wife Mary-Joelyn Schroeder (Nee Baker), also adopted two children, Mary Kathleen and Billy. I mention that because the two families occurred more like one in the real world.

Uncle Bill and my dad, though close, and running a business together, competed at almost everything else, or perhaps it was just my dad. I always got the impression that dad felt somehow deferential to Uncle Bill even though he was bigger and taller. He was the younger brother and I sort of understand that because I was now a younger brother too. My brother, Mike, was 2 years my senior and he was already there and settled in when I arrived. I would learn everything I knew about how to operate parents, from him.

Uncle Bill and my Dad were close in age and came up together in a stable family that were reasonably well off. When Uncle Bill would buy a new car, for example, Dad had to have one too. I recall when Dad pulled a two-seater Ford Thunderbird coupe, with the side porthole windows, into the driveway in response to Uncle Bill's new Pontiac Catalina station wagon, Mom was gobsmacked.

"Les, for crying out loud, you have 2 children, where are you going to put them in that thing?" She scowled. "Oh, we'll fit them in there somehow. They can ride on our laps, it'll be fine, Betty, you'll see." he pleaded. He was understandably excited to have the showpiece despite how impractical it may have been under his circumstances. Even I, at 3 years old, agreed that it was a beautiful car and in the 50s in Detroit, having such a car was quite the symbol of upward mobility. That was the prevailing energy in Detroit at the time. The booming American Auto Industry, and all the money it generated, was still based there.

Of course, the Thunderbird was a bit of a come-up from Uncle Bill's Catalina and Dad was happy about that too. Mom was undeterred, "You're going to have to take that back, Les, and get us something that we can use, for heaven's sake."

We didn't have the car for long, but Me, Dad and Mike certainly enjoyed it while we had it. Me and Mike could easily fit in the passenger seat, together. Seat Belts had not been invented yet. Little did we know how much potential danger we may have been in. Automobile dashboards were still made of steel and airbags hadn't even been thought of yet.

That dazzlingly sporty little showpiece was eventually replaced with a 2 tone Crown Victoria, which I had fallen asleep in the rear window of, many times. Even new cars, back then, would vibrate with those huge gas guzzling V-8 engines and primitive motor mounts. It wouldn't take much of a car ride for the gentle massage to put me right down. Mom and Dad would usually leave me there, baking under the sun, in the driveway until I woke up on my own; no doubt, because they could take a break from my youthful exuberance. That exuberance got me a couple of trips to the emergency room at a very tender age.

***

In Detroit, it was common to have a basement with windows that would be below ground level. Window wells opened a little bit of space so light and air could filter to the basement. While rough-housing with my brother in the driveway one day, I fell into the window well right there next to the Crown Victoria I would often fall asleep in. At least I hope I tumbled through that window rather than learning that my brother had pushed me.

Mom was already in the basement as I came crashing through the window into the laundry sink. Evidently there were several cuts that needed to be addressed, mostly on my head. I proceeded to drive my poor Mom crazy with my picking at them all the time while they were trying to heal.

***

The lines between the two budding Schroeder families was blurry at best. Uncle Bill and his family lived a little over a block away, on Shelbourne Court. Mike and I would spend a lot of time there with our cousins, who shortly thereafter included newborn Danny. Bill and Les, along with Lee and Dee Demuelemiester, jointly owned and operated A Hotel, Nightclub & Bowling Alley complex called Clinton Gables in Mt Clemens. Although it's gone now, it was enough of a draw in its day to have the likes of Rosemary Clooney headline for New Years Eve at the height of her career.

I loved being at Clinton Gables, one of the reasons was because of a big, beautiful fountain in the park right next to the Bowling Alley. There was a sculpture in the center of a big pool that had little cherubs around it that were peeing in the water. I loved playing there in the summer. It was kind of sad, in the fall, however, because they would turn the water off and drain it to clean it, I suppose. But it always seemed so sad when it was dormant. It wouldn't be that way for long, though. Once it started to snow, even though the fountain wasn't live, it would regain a different kind of beauty under a blanket of Michigan snow.

Mike and I were trained right from the beginning about things like dressing ourselves with dignity, not putting our elbows on the table, shutting up when adults are talking, saying "Please" and "Thank you" and addressing adults with Ma'am and Sir. We were being groomed to take our place among the well to do of Detroit society. That required meticulous care and strict codes of behavior. Putting my elbows on the dinner table would elicit a pinch from my mom, or maybe the threat of being stabbed with a fork from my dad.

We were Catholic, but in name only. There was church on

CHAPTER 1

Sunday, of course, and we would have to dress in our Sunday best because the people on our community expected it. There would be prayers at the foot of our beds at night before climbing in, but it was all for show.

While Mike didn't take to it all that well, I was quite effeminate in demeanor and took to it with aplomb. It appears that I have always been gay; I was just the last one in my family to accept it.

Every once in a while, as a kid, I would get weirdly impulsive and do something insanely out of character to break out of that rigid mold. Kathy, Mike and I were in the park having an engaged discussion about what would happen if we pulled the fire alarm on the streetlight pole over there by the street that ran in front of Clinton Gables.

We were all curious about it, so I walked over in the direction of the pole it was mounted on. It was a ways off, so Kathy and Mike, remaining at the fountain, had time to frantically shout their pleadings with me not to do it. I was ignoring their cautions. We all wanted to know. I don't know how I was able to reach that box at my height, but somehow, I did pull the alarm. It was silent, so I thought the coast was clear and headed proudly back to the fountain. Mike and Kathy were both watching in horror. Perhaps they knew something I didn't.

I had almost reached the fountain when the sirens began to wail. The Fire Station must have been awfully close because it was only seconds after I pulled the alarm. I hadn't even gotten to the fountain where we had been playing when the fire trucks pulled up, lights flashing and sirens wailing.

It seemed like there were a *lot* of emergency vehicles converging on the park. Mike and Kathy were squirming with worry that the hammer would come down on *them* along with me. Both pointed to me within seconds as our parents came rushing out of the bowling alley to see what was happening. Mom and Dad spared nothing in their efforts to make sure I was aware of the seriousness of what I had just done.

Aunt Jo, always the first one to take charge of a situation, rushed over to the firemen to explain and apologize profusely. It turned out that Clinton Gables had to pay for the false alarm. At least that's what Aunt Jo told me.

***

Aunt Jo was a beautiful, shapely woman with bottled blonde hair. I wouldn't learn that she was naturally a brunette until I was in my teens. She showed me a picture of herself while she was engaged to Uncle Bill. She was smart as a whip and comedy came easy to her. There was no question that she was in charge of that branch of the Schroeder family. In fact, she was at least partly in charge of ours too. My Mom was an Aquarius and not exactly the model of a modern mother. She had always traded on her looks and, as luck would have it, she had plenty of raw materials to work with, in that regard.

***

When I was that young, I would often get compliments on my manners and my diction. I assume there was a good reason for it. If not, then it wasn't for lack of trying. I ordinarily relished behaving myself, so this mess I had gotten us all into was shocking to the entire family. The gist of the admonitions I got for it was "What, in God's name were you thinking? Why did you do that?" I still don't have an answer. I don't think I'll ever know the answer to that question. I was a little kid, for crying out loud, how would I know? This kind of thing was usually in my brother's wheelhouse.

***

I spent a lot of time at Grandma Hutch's tiny but beautifully appointed cottage on Maple Street. We got along famously. There was something about me that delighted her. Grandma Hutch was a Welcome Wagon Ambassador and was the physical embodiment of the June Cleaver model. She was the type to get up before Grandpa Louie to fix her hair and face before climbing back into bed to wait for him to wake up. She was always meticulously groomed and well dressed. Mom was just like her. They were very close and the apple had not fallen far from the tree.

I only remember Grandpa Louie as being quite old, sickly and bedridden. There was only one incident that I can recall about him. I was alone with him in his room one afternoon. He asked me to show him my wee-wee. Grandma Hutch happened to appear at the bedroom door at just that moment and gently chided him about it while quickly gathering me up and escorting me from the room. I had no way to understand what was happening, just then, but I have to admire Grandma Hutch's restraint. Had that been allowed to continue, there's no way that would not have turned out badly. It was shortly after that that Grandpa Louie passed away. At the funeral home I was extremely uncomfortable about the whole affair and would not go near his opened coffin, despite mom's urging. I'm *still* creeped out about the whole subject of death.

***

Life on Colonial Court was as close as I have ever come to an idyllic existence. I'm told, I lived at the corner of Colonial Court and Mack Avenue for a while, but I couldn't swear to it. Having seen the house as an adult, I still couldn't attest to it. I have no memory of it at all, but my cousin, Kathy, and my brother, Mike, insist that's where I was brought into the Schroeder Family from the orphanage. The house around the bend from it was the one that I remember. All three of us agree that was our home for the bulk of the time before the divorce.

Growing up with my brother for the few years we were together was pendulous most of the time. I was loved and protected as well as routinely terrorized. Mike seemed to think of me as his personal toy. A toy he cherished like no other, but a toy, nonetheless. It was OK for him to mess with me until I was in tears or chase me around the house or bowling alley until I was a driveling mess. But, let anyone else even look at me cross eyed and he would spring into action putting himself between me and trouble, like a superhero.

Mike was the first kid in our family to do almost everything. Being two years older, he was the first to ride a bike without training wheels, the first to get to stay up late, the first to go to school and the first to shock the adults by cursing and swearing. He was the first one to learn how to "flip the bird" and wasted no time teaching all of that to his willing baby brother.

I've always found it funny how Mom & Dad routinely used such words when they were drinking, yet scratched their heads in wonder, trying to figure out who taught it to us. As luck would have it, one of the few luxuries of being the youngest is being blameless for using foul language at such a tender age. The response will invariably be laughter, followed by hell to pay for whoever tutored the offending language.

Mike ended up on the losing end of some relatively terse pronouncements the first time the folks heard me call him a "Shit-Ass". Mom & Dad's disdained scowling would skip over me and be leveled directly at Mike. His guilt and embarrassment were what little revenge I could exact upon him for all the terrorizing he did. His guilty face was a priceless reward.

***

One particularly active day we were rough-housing around and Mike ended up in the downstairs bathroom off the hallway just outside the kitchen. I was in the hallway taunting Mike about something. Mom was in the kitchen absent-mindedly admonishing us to quiet down, as if it was an automatic parental response to noise, rather than something she actually expected us to do.

CHAPTER 1

Mike was in the bathroom opening the door just enough to call me a name and then slamming the door shut to prevent any response I might have. One of those times, I gave him the finger right in his face, which, at that moment, was right at the door jamb. As he had been doing, he slammed the door, this time catching my middle finger in the door jamb. It took me a second to realize what was happening, but my finger began to bleed. The door had split my finger open. As would be expected, I began to scream bloody murder as I realized that my finger was bleeding quite a lot.

Mom, hearing my outburst, came running. In hindsight, I don't think she knew what to do because she immediately filled up the sink with cold water and stuck my hand in it. It didn't stop the bleeding even a little bit, so she grabbed a handful of paper towels from the kitchen and hustled me and Mike off to the hospital.

Once there, I'm pretty sure I was feeling pain, rather than the shock of seeing my finger in such a state. It took Mom and a nurse a minute to finally calm me down so the doctor could sew my finger back together. It must have been a pretty bad injury as I still carry the scar all these decades later.

Mike, meanwhile, was standing off to the side watching and, I would imagine, feeling awfully guilty. Suddenly, I shouted, "You did this to me you Shit-ass!" Mom and the doctor were taken aback by my outburst, while Mike just groaned and rolled his eyes. I think he was beginning to realize just how much trouble he was going to be in when we got back home.

Later that night as we had gone through our nightly rituals of brushing our teeth, going to the bathroom, saying our prayers and getting tucked in; Mike came over to my bed and just stood there for a minute. I could only see his silhouette against the light in the hallway shining through the half open bedroom door. He was very sincere. He said something soothing, though

I don't remember what. I could tell he felt badly about what had happened.

I knew that he would never intentionally do anything to cause me any real harm. He was my brother, for crying out loud. It simply wasn't in his nature. By this time I had calmed down considerably, aided no doubt, by some chemical persuasion prescribed by the doctor earlier that day. Although I couldn't swear to it, I think I forgave him. He leaned down and hugged me, just for a second and scampered back to his bed. From then on, he seemed a little more careful and a little more attentive to me for the longest time.

***

One of the things I took to early in life was Ice Skating. There was a rink nearby that we went to sometimes. Mike wasn't satisfied with having to share the rink with everyone, so he rigged one in our back yard, one winter. He talked Dad into shoveling all the snow in the back yard into a big circle. Mike pulled out our garden hose and dragged it over to the circle and filled it with water. He and I immediately went in the house and waited with our noses pressed up against the dining room window, for our new ice rink to freeze so we could get out there and play. It couldn't freeze quickly enough for us. It took a while before we came to the realization that patience was a thing.

The next day, it was frozen and we were so excited to get out there. Mike, of course, had his trusty Hockey skates and was already in pretty good control of them. Calling what I had a pair of skates, was stretching the definition a bit. They were 2 blades a few inches apart that I strapped on to the soles of my boots somewhat like the rudimentary metal roller skates that were common for kids at the time. The stability of the two blades, rather than one, kept me upright most of the time and I was in heaven. There is something romantic about gliding around without having to move my legs that really appealed to me. It felt like I would imagine a bird feels and it kept my mind busy along with the rest of me.

Our little private skating rink didn't last long as freezing and thawing is, sadly, a reality in Michigan winters. Within a day or two, Mike and I were back at the neighborhood rink accidentally slamming into other kids and trying to pick ourselves back up and get back in there.

I think that rink has stuck with me all those years because I maintained an interest in skating, both on wheels and blades for the remainder of my childhood, even though all of the other stuff I was going through. It was like a romance with gracefulness. Grace is not something that would otherwise describe anything about me; then *or* now. I'm a Taurus and the things you learn about Taurus describe me to a "T". Well intentioned as I may have been, I have always been a bull in a China shop. I was clumsy, awkward, and oblivious to all of it. I still don't care what I look like while enveloped in my romantic love of all things graceful. It would surely harshen how it all felt, and how it felt was everything to me.

***

For a very few years, I was truly living a kid's life. If only more of my childhood could have been like those first few of years with the Schroeders. It was just about the only period in my life that would feel "Normal" to me; whatever that means. But I did get to have that care-free love and joy for a little while, at least! Not the least of which was because of my brother Mike. He seemed to take no small amount of delight in having me as a little brother.

CHAPTER 2

Clinton Gables

All of us kids loved hanging out at the bowling alley at Clinton Gables. We knew the place better than our own homes. We didn't have a nanny. Our parents watched over us while at work, so we knew the bowling alley well. Meanwhile, the parents tended to the serious business of bowling, socializing with the customers and drinking huge quantities of beer. I assume they occasionally took time out to actually run the business, but I was seldom nearby when that happened.

The bowling alley had two levels, one on top of the other. The top level was usually closed to the public unless there were leagues going on. Part of the upper lanes could be seen from the bowling counter, through a metal railing. That's where Mike, Kathy, Billy and I spent most of our time, where we couldn't get in anyone's way. It was also where I got my first taste of beer.

I must have been four at the time. That would mean that Mike was six. There was a bar on each level of the bowling alley and my brother, older and wiser guy that he was knew from watching the folks that if you pulled that lever right there, beer would come out.

We knew all too well that beer was not for children, so naturally, our interest in trying it was piqued. Mike was sitting on the bar stool next to me, we were resting after a vigorous game of running up and down the approach lanes and jumping over the ball returns.

Mike was practically my opposite in appearance. Short, thin and already somewhat sinewy, he was almost completely covered with bright gold freckles. He sported short wavy red hair that he seldom ever combed, and the clearest light blue eyes I have seen to this day. He carried himself with that classic little boy "Aw, Shucks" kind of a manner and seemed to be completely unflappable. He resembled Mickey Rooney for the entirety of his life. Even as they both aged. I do not recall him ever being angry or upset by anything. Perhaps I was angry and upset enough for both of us. Between the two of us, I was the whiner.

As we sat there on two of the bar stools, he was explaining, in his best "Big Brother" fashion, how the draught tap worked. I was enraptured with his great knowledge while he was thoroughly enjoying his position of being my big brother.

Suddenly the look on his face changed and the tone of his voice became quiet and decidedly conspiratorial. He was about to involve me in something secret and only he and I, and no one else, could ever know, not even our cousins.

Then, quietly and with a serious tone, he admitted to me that he had actually filled a glass from the tap downstairs. "Yeah", he said, "Dad was showing me how to do it for when we grow up and have to run this place." "Wanna see me do it for real?", "No, Mike, we'll get in trouble", I cautioned. "Oh, come on Greg, we'll just pour a little tiny bit in this glass and then we'll drink it so no one will know we did it". I continued to resist for a while but soon enough, I was as excited as he was about this terrible thing we could do and completely get away with.

Mike climbed up on the bar and positioned himself carefully next to the tap. He put the glass up to the spout and looked at me for a moment as if to say "Well, Greg, here goes nothing!" He paused for just a second and then pulled the lever down and then quickly back up. It made, what seemed like, a huge sound that caught us both by surprise. We froze like we had just been caught by the police in the course of a robbery.

We frantically looked in every direction at once to see if anyone heard the noise and was coming after us. When our hearts started beating at a relatively normal pace and we were sure no one heard us pour the beer, Mike brought the glass, with a couple inches of beer in it, back down to the stool and held it reverently between us.

"Now, if I drink some of this beer, you have to too", he said, and looked me straight in the eye as if this was the most important and sacred pact any two people could ever make. "OK", I said. "You gotta promise", he cautioned, "and swear to God you'll never tell anyone we did this." Mike paused for effect, "Not even *Kathy*!!!" Oh my God, he was bringing out the big guns now!

Kathy was my total confidant; we were the tightest. Our parents all called us the "Kissing Cousins" because of how close we were. I couldn't imagine keeping a secret from her. However, this was evidently serious business, so I made an exception. Besides, we were pretty much at the point of no return. The beer was already poured, and Mike was holding it in his hand as we were talking.

Mike waited silently while I made up my mind. "OK, I swear." Convinced that all the precautions necessary to pull off such a criminal act were seen to, Mike ceremoniously took a sip from the glass, and then another. As he handed the glass to me, he let out that sharp exhaled "AAAH!" sound like they do in the cowboy movies whenever anyone takes a drink, and watched with abated breath.

I took the glass and moved it up to my lips. I could already sense that familiar beer smell. Not only was it all around us when we were here at the bowling alley, but it was a smell we were all too familiar with on our folks and Aunt Jo and Uncle Bill. I tilted the glass and let the beer flow into my mouth. I think I sort of liked it but the thing I remember the most about the taste of it was that it seemed way too serious for someone my age. It felt weird and tingly, and the aftertaste was not very pleasant. Suddenly I felt compelled to erase the entire affair from existence, but it was too late.

I could sense that Mike was experiencing some regret as well. We just sat there for a moment wallowing in our private guilt, in marked contrast to the exhilaration we had felt just moments ago while planning this dastardly deed.

Finally, without a word, Michael climbed down from the stool and walked around behind the bar to the sink, where he began to wash the glass. As he did so we heard footsteps on the stairs leading up to the upper level. We froze again, only this time it was not a false alarm. It was Dad. His first words were the very words we were dreading the most at that moment. "What are you two knuckleheads up to here?" he said in a lighthearted manner, with that alcohol induced smile that we would come to know so well.

Dad was generally a casual sort, usually good-natured and ruggedly handsome in his way. He was big and not quite fat. He carried himself with a confident masculinity that was a good part of his charm. I remember him as highly excitable at times, given to verbal tirades at the drop of a hat, but almost never physically violent with us. He had jet black hair that he combed straight back, and large, piercing black eyes like mine. In his appearance and manner, he reminded me a lot of a younger, thinner, Jackie Gleason.

There he stood at the top of the stairs, about 20 or 30 feet from us. We could only see his outline because the mid-day sun shining through the glass brick wall behind him was the only light in the room. He was waiting for an answer. I looked at Mike with guilt written all over my face. "What do we do now?" I thought, "Get us out of this mess, please Mike!!!" I was on the verge of peeing my pants, I was so scared.

Finally, my brother rescued the situation. "We're playing

bartender," he said, "What'll ya' have Partner?" Without missing a beat, Dad fell into the game Mike had just created. "Gimme a draught, Barkeep," he said. He sauntered over to us with an exaggerated swagger, like a cowboy in the movies sidling up to the bar in an old west saloon. He plopped himself down on the stool next to me and squeezed my knee with a good-natured wink. Mike and I looked at each other, breathless for a moment, not quite sure whether he was on to us.

Mike stood on a case of empty long necks and lifted the very glass we just drank our first taste of beer from. He lifted it up to the tap and grabbed the lever. My heart stood still wondering if he was really going to pull the lever or just pretend. "TSHHHHHHH," he mimicked the sound of drawing a beer, and I immediately began to breathe.

I was so relieved that he didn't pull that lever like he had done just moments ago. I no longer felt compelled to pee my pants either. But, as Mike was pretending to draw the beer, Dad nodded at him and said, "Go ahead, Son." Mike looked at him, not quite sure he heard him right. "Really," he asked? "Yeah," Dad said, "draw me a beer like I showed you." Sheepishly, Mike pulled the lever and filled the glass. Then he smiled broadly as he slid the glass across the bar in front of Dad.

I was sometimes jealous of the rapport between my brother and my Dad, they were both very masculine and confident in themselves and shared a lot of common interests. Dad was somewhat of a sportsman, and liked fishing, hunting and camping and such. Mike caught on to those things early on and developed a real interest that he nurtured throughout his life.

I, on the other hand, was very effeminate and a city kid to the core. I couldn't be bothered with the great outdoors. I was into singing and dancing and pretending to be Liberace in front of the living room picture window curtain and hanging around with Mom while Dad and Mike did "Guy Stuff".

After a few minutes more of the bartender game, Dad got serious and started talking to us about something or other. I don't remember exactly what he talked about, but I remember that it was one of those moments we had when I felt very close to both of them. Dad was probably beginning to prepare us for the divorce that was soon to come. During this conversation, Dad hugged us a couple of times, and may have even told us that he loved us. I don't recall whether he said it, but I was feeling it loud and clear.

When Dad had finally finished his beer, he picked us both up, one under each arm and proceeded to carry us downstairs. Mike and I looked at each other across the expanse of Dad's body as he carried us and smiled at one another. We had, indeed, gotten away with drinking our first taste of beer.

CHAPTER 3

Hall of the Divine Child

The first school I went to, and I have precious little memory of it, was Our Lady Star of the Sea. It was, of course, a Catholic School. My Cousin Kathy insists that that is where I started my schooling and I have no case to argue against it. However, the first school I do remember going to was a Catholic Military Academy called Hall of the Divine Child in Monroe. I was in first grade.

I was a problem child to Les & Betty that early in my life. Well, to be honest, it was mostly my dad. Not that I had done anything wrong, but because my demeanor, my behavior, was decidedly effeminate. At the time, being gay was considered a pretty big problem. Both of the young Schroeder Families came from upper middle-class money. Grandpa Schroeder was in steel at the height of the Auto Industry in Detroit. The Bakers, Aunt Jo's Parents, were in real estate development, Grandpa Louie and Grandma Hutch, mom's parents, were importers of fine China from Europe before my Grandpa died. One brand of which was their namesake: Hutchenreuther!

The expectation on the two Schroeder families to be successful and take their place among the elite of Detroit's high society was practically bred into them. In that environment me, and my girlish demeanor, stuck out like a sore thumb. Homosexuality was still listed in the Diagnostic Manual of Mental Disorders, as a mental disorder that needed attention before it set in and became an embarrassment to my family. Of course, there were gay people in high society at the time. There always have been. But in the 50s it was all kept rigidly under wraps. I didn't fit that mold, even a little bit.

Military school was the chosen solution that was supposed to turn me into a boy. Mike, being a normal boy already, stayed behind with Mom & Dad. I was taken to Hall of the Divine Child.

It was quite the beautiful campus. It was quiet and peaceful with a few meditative spaces scattered about where we would often see, the sisters or brothers, praying a rosary or reading quietly. There was a long narrow pond with a beautiful bridge over it. If it froze over enough during the winter, some of us would skate on it.

One winter afternoon when mom and my brother came to visit, they had brought me a brand-new pair of single blade skates complete with those protective rubber blade covers. I was beside myself with excitement. We were relaxing by the pond, and I couldn't help myself. I immediately put the skates on and put them to use. Evidently, not all the ice was thick enough to hold me and it wasn't long before I went through.

Mike, always my protector and knowing I couldn't swim, sprang into action and splayed himself out on the ice and inched his way over to the hole I had just disappeared into. He reached down into the icy water and grabbed me by one of the arms I was flailing around just under the surface. He quickly pulled me up just enough so I could climb out of danger. I was wet and shivering cold, but I refused to take those skates off. I was already deeply in love with them. Mom and Mike helped me put the skate guards on and led me back to the school so I could dry off and change into a fresh uniform.

***

A lasting memory I have of Hall of the Divine Child was being in the infirmary and being sicker than I had ever been before. I was having a bizarre dream that seemed to go on forever repeating itself. I remember the dream. There was this wide hallway with doors on either side of it, facing one another. There were strings, or wires or something that ran across the hallway from one door to the one across from it. I was seeing this scene from below the hallway, as if the floor had been made of glass and I was trapped beneath it. There were mice or something that kept scampering back and forth along the lines. I felt so horrible, physically, and I couldn't stop the dream from repeating itself over and over. I was evidently delirious.

The Nuns had me moved to a day room by myself. The windows were open, and it was warm and sunny outside. While in the day room I remember being visited by My Mom and my brother, they were tearful during our visit. They were telling me that I was sick, which I knew, and that they were concerned about me. Then, a day or so later, my Aunt Jo & Uncle Bill visited along with my cousins. Most of them were crying too. Looking back, I would guess that some-one, or some-thing, had given them the impression that I was on my death bed. Since I'm telling the story many decades later, the evidence would suggest that I was not.

I still don't know what that illness may have been. None of the records I have even mention it, but I suspect it was Rheumatic Fever. Rheumatic Fever is rare and was considered potentially fatal at the time. The reason I suspected Rheumatic Fever is because I had a heart murmur well into my thirties. It was the reason I was classified 4-F in the Military Draft for the War in Viet Nam. At the time, every boy was required to register for the draft when they turned 18. Part of the registration process included a physical exam. During that exam, my heart murmur was noticed. I, quite literally, dodged a bullet because of it.

One of my classmates was a cadet named Michael Morrison. While at Hall of the Divine Child, Morrison and I had little interaction with one another, other than being classmates. He would later come into play at another Catholic military academy years later. What I didn't know at the time was that his dad, an injured Military Officer, was also the drill Sergeant for HDC. He taught us military decorum and Junior ROTC. He was always in uniform, and it was easy to see that Morrison had not fallen far from the tree.

His Dad was somewhat wiry and not unusually tall. When we cadets misbehaved or failed to perform properly, he would grab us by the head and quickly lift us off the floor about a foot or so and drop us. It was his way of getting our attention.

It sounds much worse when I say it than it was to experience it. It was actually a little endearing. Many times, I would feel his firm but gentle hands on either side of my head, cupping my ears, quickly hoisting my little frame and dropping me because he didn't like how I stood at attention. My "Parade Rest" left a bit to be desired, as well. I tended to be girlishly lackadaisical about it. At one time or another all of us had experienced this technique. Truth be told, it was almost comical, and it did get the job done.

***

One day, while I was still at HDC, my dad showed up unannounced. I don't know this to be true, but I suspect that he was checking to see if military school had turned me into a boy yet. We spent the better part of the day together and it was as uncomfortable as it usually was when we found ourselves alone together. He took me to see the Monroe waterfalls. They were a long series of carefully neat, identical waterfalls made of cement that ran through Monroe. The city was quite proud of them and for good reason. They were very beautiful and calming. They were lined with flower beds and benches so people could leisurely enjoy the whole scene. Dad bought us both a sandwich and we had lunch together. Of Course, I was begging to come home with him, but he kept redirecting the conversation to something else. His marriage was in more trouble than was visible to me or Mike and I'm sure that was by design that he kept it from us.

It wasn't long after dad's visit that it was decided that I'd be taken to the cabin up north to live with Grandma Schroeder, Aunt Fifi and Grandma Tini. Evidently, my girlish behavior had already set in, or hopefully, my parents had settled with the fact that my behavior was just how I actually was and couldn't be trained out of me. I can only imagine how uncomfortable things could have gotten if they hadn't given up on trying to change me into somebody else.

CHAPTER 4

The Cabin Up North

Mom & Dad weren't getting along very well. They kept it away from us, thankfully, but their marriage was about to dissolve. Mike and I, being adopted, was evidently part of a plan to rescue what was a failing second marriage for both Les & Betty. They were in their 30s when we were adopted.

Times must have been good, financially, because the whole combined family had bought a piece of lakefront land a good stretch east of Gaylord Michigan on Peanut Lake. Maybe there was life insurance involved left by Grampa Schroeder when he died. The cabin was way out there in a rural area that was a haven for fishing and hunting.

Dad & Uncle Bill were building a cabin on the property for their mother, Grandma Schroeder, to live in year around while either, and/or both younger Schroeder families could also vacation there. We did that quite a bit. Grandma Schroeder was then living with Aunt Fifi and Grandma Tini a few blocks from us in Detroit where Grandma & Grandpa Schroeder had lived when he was still alive. Grandma Schroeder wanted to get out of the city. It reminded her too much of Grandpa Schroeder, I would imagine.

There were many wonderful weeks up north in that Cabin. Not the least of which was building that 7-bedroom behemoth. My brother, my cousins and I were very young, but we were helping with little things that little people could do. I would later live there for several months while Mom and Dad were dissolving their marriage. The cabin, I learned much later, was the scene of some of the more unsavory intermingling among the adults which led to the irreconcilable differences cited by Mom & Dad in their divorce. Evidently none of the adults in our families were as "Catholic" as they let on.

During construction, no bathrooms existed yet. The cabin was nothing more than a cement slab, a little bigger than a Basketball Court, at that point. Uncle Bill built us a toilet. Not an outhouse, mind you, a toilet just barely blinded by foliage. He had twisted a coat hanger into a makeshift toilet paper dispenser and nailed it to a nearby tree. He pieced together a wooden box at roughly the right height for kids and adults, both, and cut an appropriately sized hole in the top. That was our bathroom in its entirety. It had to be moved every once in a while to a fresh location while the previous hole in the ground would be covered over with dirt. It was a lake-front property, so bathing was not a problem. Nor was fresh water.

We lived in a camper trailer on the property during construction. To us Kids, it was fun, but Mom and Aunt Jo were not the least bit amused and spared no language in expressing their displeasure. They eventually did become accustomed to it, but not without some colorful remarks about the less than 5-star accommodations. They certainly didn't like the "Bathroom" much.

It was a big and beautiful place about 20 yards up the hill from Peanut Lake. The folks had placed a salt lick within easy walking distance of the cabin so it would be an easy trek to spy on the deer that would come looking for it. The Salt Lick was probably positioned there so my Dad and Uncle Bill could lure the deer close enough to the cabin so they wouldn't have far to travel to shoot them, though they never did while I was around. The youngsters, me included, would have thrown a fit if they had. We were busy trying in vain to make friends with the deer.

I got my education about fishing from Dad and my brother. It was the centerpiece of their bonding. Dad and Mike both loved the outdoors and the whole world of fishing and hunting. Mike taught me how to make a fish scaler out of a piece of wood onto which he had nailed a couple rows of beer bottle caps that were cast aside by our parents. He taught me how to rub the dead fish against the grain of their scales to remove them before we fried them. Even at that young age, he could tell you by sight what genus a freshwater fish it was. Perch, Bass, Trout. Mackerel and a bunch more that I might have known back then but have long since forgotten. Fishing was never my thing.

Dad, Mike and Uncle Bill found no small amount of humor in my discomfort about handling dead fish. But I felt so close to Mike during these few moments. He dearly loved teaching me things even if I had little interest in learning them. It was like I was visiting him in *his* world, and he seemed to like that. I had to admit that his love of all that was infectious, even to me.

We had a canoe that we kept on top of the garage that we launched from a short dock that Dad and Uncle Bill had built. The cabin was up the hill from the lake, so my dad and uncle dug some troughs in the sloping soil and laid wooden beams in them to form a kind of staircase leading down to the dock. Birch tree roots close to the surface of the ground provided a few of the steps.

From the cabin, you could see down the corridor between the birch trees, all the way to the dock. There was lots of swimming too. The water was clear and shallow enough that you could see the bottom and every little creature that lived there. My favorites were the minnows. We used to catch them with a net and keep them in a bucket of water to use for bait for the bigger fish. It seemed like there were millions of them. I spent many hours laying on that dock looking down into the water watching the marine life going about their business.

I learned how to swim there. We had taken the canoe around the bend to the Billings' dock. I had never met the Billings, but I'm guessing that the adults knew them at least in passing. Dad, Mom, Aunt Jo &, Mike were swimming in the water, and I was standing on the dock, crying because I couldn't swim. Well, I *could* swim; I just didn't know it while I was standing there on the dock whining about not being able to.

Mike, already in the water, was trying to explain the dog paddle to me and showing me how to keep my head above the water and the rest of the family was unified in their encouragement for me to stop crying and just jump in. I wanted to and I'm sure they could see it. I was missing out on something that was obviously a lot of fun for them.

They were all right there in the water and insistent that they wouldn't let me drown, but I wasn't having it. Finally, my Dad, impatient with my whining, climbed the ladder up to the dock, walked over to me, picked me up and just tossed me off the end of the dock without a word.

It turned out that I *could* swim, after all. With little involvement from the rest of the family, I immediately started Dog Paddling like I had been doing it my whole life. They were all watching in anticipation, ready to intervene if needed. Although I was in a state of complete panic, once I was in the water my panic slowly dissolved and was replaced with an excited sense of accomplishment,,, and Dog Paddling.

Dad and I were never close. That was reserved for him and Mike and their hunting and fishing. My effeminate behavior unnerved my dad so there was rarely a time when he and I would ever be alone together. During our short life together, I always felt like it was all my dad could do to grudgingly tolerate how I behaved.

Mike would sometimes drag me down to the lake plop me down

in the canoe and paddle out to the middle of the small lake and we would fish. I would occasionally catch one or two, with his able assistance, but I never developed an interest in it. I'd have much preferred to play Jacks or Marbles on a playground somewhere. I was pretty good at both. It was my superpower on a playground.

Those times out there on the lake with my brother stick with me because of his love for me and his love of fishing. But try as he might, he never could get me to catch on to his love of the great out-doors. I would always complain of being bored. He so enjoyed his times with Dad, and I think he was secretly trying his best to get me included. Maybe he figured that it would get dad to the point where he could see in me what Mike did. I don't know.

Later, that cabin, along with Grandma Schroeder, Aunt Fifi and Grandma Tini, would be my home too. It was right after I got back from Hall of the Divine Child. The cabin was finished and we had all been enjoying it for a while. Grandma Schroeder was clearly in charge of our little family. She was a forward looking 40s kind of woman with a slight frame and curly brown hair. She loved her coffee and Pall Mall straights. She made coffee every day with a weathered glass pour-over coffee maker. She would fold a big round filter paper in 4ths and form the cone that fit perfectly in the coffee beaker. It was a whole ritual that she did every time in the same order.

I liked watching her cut the ends from those big 5lb metal coffee cans. She would flatten them with the lids tucked inside. She did that with all the cans. Being so far from a grocery store, most of our food was in cans, so there were a lot of them. There was a rack with a stack of the flattened cans by the back door. Maybe it was a habit she had that came from saving tin for the war effort. Recycling wasn't a thing yet.

Grandma Schroeder had a kind motherly demeanor and I think

she really liked my swishy little girlishness. She was in the right job for sure. Aunt Fifi was a little taller and thin as a rail. She sported long white hair that was always in a French twist. She was the loud, funny one, hailing from Bay City. I really didn't know the story about how she came to be included in this trio. I only assume that she was Grandma Schroeder's sister because all of us called her Aunt Fifi. I always felt like there was a story there, but I never learned what it was. She was just Aunt Fifi who was always up on celebrity gossip.

While I lived there, we did a lot of bonding over Photoplay, Hollywood Confidential, Soap Opera Digest & Modern Screen Magazines. There were a handful of others as well, but all of them are gone now. That was her joy! She would thoroughly scour them all, almost like it was her job. The original Guiding Light was her favorite Soap. Everything had to stop when that show came on. How they were able to get a Television Signal way out there is beyond me, but somehow, they did.

Grandma Tini was the Mystery lady. She was big in every direction, much older than the others and walked like she was walking on eggshells, often with a walker. She stayed in her room most of the time; no doubt because it was such a chore for her to get up and move around. She was not a well woman. There is also evidence that she may have been in the early stages of Dementia or Alzheimer's. She would do and say weird things a lot.

The distance between our cabin and Gaylord Michigan was quite a trek. I don't know how far it is in miles, but it seemed like at least a half hour drive, maybe even a little more. The last half of the trip was on a narrow, bumpy dirt road. One time when we were returning from town, Grandma Schroeder was sitting next to Aunt Fifi in the front seat of their big old Plymouth. The kind that looks like a gargantuan gas guzzling bubble made from steel. Theirs was brown.

CHAPTER 4

In the back seat was me, Grandma Tini, Kathy, Billy, and Mike. We were already well into the trip, and I had to pee. I held it for a while and finally began talking about it out loud, which brought on a lively dissertation from the front seat including an education in communicating things at the appropriate time, and an interrogation about what I might have been thinking about or doing while we were in town instead of going to the bathroom.

Grandma Tini, tiring of the discussion, and my bouncing up and down clutching my little crotch, motions me to pee on the floorboard, which I did, without seeking a second opinion from any of the others. I really didn't want one. I was laser-focused on the business at hand and I had Grandma Tini's permission.

In the back seat there's now a whole new discussion going on. This one is silent. Grandma Tini is holding her finger up to her lips and trying to muffle her giggling. Mike, Kathy and Billy are in various degrees of horror, laughter and shock and begin whispering just loud enough to alert Grandma Schroeder and Aunt Fifi, up front, that something had happened. Aunt Fifi turned back to us demanding to know what's going on.

Meanwhile, in the back seat, we are climbing all over each other trying not to step in the puddle which is now sloshing pack and forth across the floorboard. Grandma Schroeder and Aunt Fifi turned their attention to Grandma Tini and had even more questions. Grandma Tini was often doing and saying weird things like that when she wasn't in her room, which led me to think, now, that maybe she wasn't firing on all cylinders.

***

While I lived up north with these women, I met a man who also lived in the area year around. I don't recall his name but I'm going to call him "Earl". If his name wasn't Earl, he looked like he probably *should* have been named Earl. His little place in the world was within walking distance of our cabin. He was older, with just barely graying brown, wavy hair and a gruff but kind manner.

Earl and I just talked a lot about nothing, and he seemed like he knew everything, compared to me anyway. He would have me help him with stuff like catching minnows, stocking the wood cradle and filling the Kerosene lamp. He was patient and kind with plenty of witty remarks and a solid handful of "Dad Jokes" from Reader's Digest, ready at hand.

He was my first exposure to a radical non-conformist. Of course, I didn't know what that meant at the time, but I *did* know that I was stepping into a whole other world when I was there; a world very different than my own. He was disconnected from what little grid existed in the 50s. He didn't even have a phone and I doubt that there was an address yet for properties way out there. Everybody living out there seemed to know each other.

I spent time with Earl at his little cabin now and then. Grandma Schroeder knew him so my visiting him by myself didn't ruffle a feather with her. She was probably happy to have me out of her hair for those occasional visits.

Earl's cabin had a little covered porch and a genuine feel of old school living to it. A wood stove sat a little away from one wall, no doubt to warm bitter cold of winters in central Michigan. He was a fisher and hunter too. Lots of tackle hung on the walls along with a couple of rifles and there was a little loft where he slept. He was using a kerosene lamp for lighting because there was no electricity; at least not that I could tell.

He was kind to me, and I enjoyed stepping into another world that was so very different from our cabin. We did have a phone and electricity. We had a nice fireplace too. It was big. It took up almost a third of the depth of the building. Earl had lots of stories and I was a good and attentive audience. He was a good enough storyteller that it didn't matter if I wasn't much interested in the subject. He was the story.

My time, living at the cabin up north was a pretty good life, though short lived. There was no school nearby, which was fine with me, but not so with the adults in my life. They all agreed that this placement wasn't going to be a long-term solution for what to do with me. This is when I began to conceptualize the possibility that my presence was, somehow, a problem that needed to be solved.

"I was doing just fine, right here!" I thought. I had my own room, the run of the whole cabin, a TV, I had my Lincoln Logs, my Erector Set, plenty of celebrity magazines and 3 wise old women who loved me and seemed happy to entertain me with stories about the family, Politics, Catholicism, Celebrity Gossip and words of wisdom. Just outside those double glass doors was nature as far as the eye can see, a canoe tethered to a private dock on a lake and nothing but time on my hands. I was doing just fine!

But sadly, it wasn't to be.

CHAPTER 5

Anchor Bay Drive

Mom and Dad separated for real. It had been coming for a while, but it was clear now, even to us kids. Les and Betty couldn't hide it anymore. We were living with Mom, who was clandestinely seeing a handsome buffed up Italian named Paul Tocco. We had seen Paul around, but he was on the peripheral of our lives as Mom was dreaming up a way to tell me and Mike that she had moved on from our dad and was beginning a new life with Paul. Finally, the time had come to tell us. Mom and Paul solemnly called us into the living room. Mike and I knew something big was about to happen and Mike, being the big brother, likely has some idea of what it was.

Paul and Mom, crouched down to our level and faced us head on, to explain that our lives were about to be upended. Everyone was crying except Paul as they explained that sometimes when people love one another, things don't work out the way they planned, and they must live apart. "That is what was happening right now", they explained. What we had known as our family, was gone now and that things would have to change. Paul and Mom needed some time together to establish their new relationship and so Mike and I would be going to live with our dad across Lake St Clair in Anchor Bay.

That hit pretty me hard! I knew that something wasn't right, but I couldn't yet conceptualize what this all meant. What I did know is that I had an attachment to my mom that Mike probably didn't have. He was easily dad's favorite. I, on the other hand was a "Momma's Boy". I remember how it would annoy her to wake up in the morning to find me standing in her doorway staring at her. When I say that out loud, I realize how creepy it sounds, but it made all the sense in the world to me. My Mom was the most beautiful woman who ever walked the earth to this little effeminate toddler. I was just enjoying her beauty like a piece of fine art.

For a time, Mike and I stayed with Dad and his new wife, Shirley Snyder. Shirley was a prettier version of the Cruella Deville character from the Disney movie, "101 Dalmatians". She carried herself with that same artistic and dramatic flair, though not quite so menacing. She even sported that white streak in her otherwise jet-black hair, just like Cruella's. In a classic movie sense, she was our wicked stepmother.

It was not a good time for me because Shirley was not a willing participant in this new family configuration, and I wasn't exactly Dad's favorite. She and my dad were clearly in love. There was no mistaking that. But Shirley had two sons of her own from a previous marriage and was not excited about the prospect of raising two more. One of her sons was grown and had already flown the nest. The other, Craig, was treated with exceptional privilege and had little contact with me and Mike.

He had his own room and Shirley wasn't very comfortable with her son hanging out with a couple of wayward orphans. Craig was older than Mike and didn't figure prominently in our lives. We were subtly discouraged from interacting very much. Our Bedroom was the porch, which had been enclosed with windows and made into a kind of day room with a clear view to the lake. I had a bed, but Mike slept on a couch about 3 feet away.

Life outside the house was fun enough. We were living in a beautiful but little house on Lake St. Clair directly across the lake from Detroit. I don't know that I lived there for very long, but a lot had happened there anyway, good and bad.

I had begun acting out by this time. Evidently the break-up affected me a lot more than it did my brother. Mike was always unflappable anyway, at least on the outside. His trauma wouldn't become apparent to me until he was a full-grown alcoholic in his forties.

My best friend on Anchor Bay Drive was a young boy named Carl Benocci. He was already a delinquent, although I never did find out what he was acting out about. He had what appeared to be a stable loving family that was fully intact. He was just another kid who lived nearby, and we tolerated each other's weirdness with nary a ripple. He was my size and shape, but although white, he had olive skin, jet black hair and coal black eyes. He was quick and creative. I think the thing I liked about him the most was his quirks. They didn't seem threatening or menacing to me. He was just weird; entertaining, perhaps.

One thing that Carl and I bonded over was our mutual love of Duck Decoys. They were wooden sculptures of ducks that hunters would float out on the lake to attract real ducks. He had several of them. Or maybe he appropriated his like I did. They were everywhere out there.

Somewhere along the timeline, I happened upon a Decoy that Mike informed me, in this usual big brother way, was a Mallard. He knew that kind of thing. Or at least he convinced me that he did. In hindsight, it must have belonged to someone, but I had repurposed it as my own. An unauthorized interdepartmental transfer, if you will. No one ever came after me about it, so I guess it was mine.

There was no beach along the lake behind the row of houses on Anchor Bay Drive. There were weathered seawalls that separated our back yards from the lake. The seawall didn't have to do much because the water was only waist deep to my little body. The seawalls had a plank on top, usually about 6 or 8 inches wide, kind of like a sidewalk. Everybody had them. Maybe it was a regulation or building code or something. These seawalls went the entire length of the jetty that our houses were lined up on.

I had tied a string to the eyelet that decoys have for attaching a lead sinker to it to keep it in place in the water. I dropped my decoy in the water along the seawall and would walk it like it was a puppy on a leash. I liked how it floated and how it left a little rooster tail behind it as I walked along pulling it behind me. Fully engrossed in my duck walking, I didn't notice that the seawall took a sharp Right turn. I did not!

The distance I fell, was a little over my height, so taking a tumble wouldn't be expected to cause any traumatic injury. However, unbeknownst to me, at the bottom of the lake, right in that spot, was a broken beer bottle from some forgotten drunken party. My left foot came down squarely on that upturned broken bottle. Dad fixed me up and I had to wear a special sock and couldn't go in the water for a while.

One of the coolest things about living on the lake was the raft that Dad had built. It was a square platform, big enough to be supported by a bunch of empty 55-gallon oil drums, each in their own little cubicle under the deck. It was solid as a rock and moored in place by a big anchor with a hefty chain. There was a fixed ladder that descended into the water to make is easy to climb on to.

Over the course of my life, I have thought about the image of that raft out there on the lake, many times. I can still see it. Depending on the weather, that raft might look spooky one day, excitedly bouncing around the next, quiet and meditative when the water is calm, or inviting me to come and play on another day, but in the image, I hold of that raft there are never any people on it. It's always out there away from the shore, all by itself; solitary and maybe a little lonely. Sometimes in my mind's eye, I see it lose its mooring and watch it drift, gently and quietly out of View. It's almost like a metaphor for how my life was unfolding.

We all spent a lot of time out there sunning and swimming and diving. I could swim out to it, but I was afraid to try it by myself. It was a ways off shore. The water, even at the raft, was shallow enough to drop anchor. It was probably no more than 8 or 10 feet. I'd wait until Mike or Craig wanted to go out there. Or maybe it was a rule that I wasn't to go out there alone. Actually, that makes a lot more sense.

Either way, I rarely had to wait long. We all loved swimming out there to hang out in the sun and dive off the platform. I could never match Craig. He looked like a pro, diving off that raft. Mike was the clown. Cannon Balls and comical attempts at flips and swan dives was his specialty. It was quite something to watch. I could much more frequently be found playing closer to the seawall, where I could stand up in the water, which was occasionally so clear that I could see the schools of minnows going about their business.

On the other side of our house, across the road from the row of homes, was a canal. Most families had boats of varying sizes from dinghies and canoes all the way up to luxury cabin cruisers. So, there were boat houses sprinkled along the canal. Some were elaborate with winches to lift the boats out of the water for the winter months.

Our boat was a simple 12-foot rowboat that we kept in the water, moored to a short dock parallel to the canal. We had pulled it out of the canal right under our dock. It must have sank at some point and was left for dead. I can just imagine some former owner gazing down into the murky canal at the sunken ruin, shaking his head, and walking away in frustration.

Me, Mike and Dad went to work pulling it back up and fixing it up to give it another life. It didn't take long either. A few days later me and Mike were out there rowing our little hearts out, nautically exploring the neighborhood.

Across the canal to the east was nothing. Well, to be exact, nothing we could see from where we were for a robust stand of Cat Tails, beyond which we guessed, was the highway that wound around the northern edge of Lake St Clair, to Detroit.

Given the time Mike and I spent rowing that boat up and down the canal, you'd think we would be a lot more buffed than our little frames had ever showed. Or maybe we were a couple of little muscle men and never gave it a thought. At the time, we were fairly occupied with the ongoing business of being kids. I have no trouble remembering how much of a job being a kid was. There was always something to spark our imaginations. It was relentlessly busy. At that age, you don't tire easily.

Mike and I had an allowance every week for doing chores at home and around the property. I think it was something like 35 cents. In 1957, I could easily have scored a bottle of pop and some candy and walked out with most of my allowance still intact.

We would boat or walk the road to the little corner store for kid type supplies. Today, I guess you'd call it a convenience store. At the time, we called it the Bait Store and everyone would know what we meant. This one had ammunition for the hunters, Bee Bees for us kids, fishing tackle and bait for the fishers along with some basic groceries and, of course, beer. It was at the junction of our street and the highway.

I'm walking out on faith here because I don't remember this at all, but Mike insists that it impacted his life enough to mention it to me some 30 years later. There was a bend in the road just before you would get to the bait store. One day, there was a small and weathered Johnson outboard trolling motor at that bend that I guess one of our neighbors was trying to sell for something like $10 dollars. At the time, that was a sizable chunk of money. This lit Mike up and I'm surprised that I don't remember it because Mike was a total delight when he was lit up about something. Think Mickey Rooney in the movie "BoysTown" with Spencer Tracy; excited, engaged and a bit of a ham.

When we got home Mike started in on Dad to get him to buy it for us. F. Lee Bailey would have been proud of the case that Mike presented to our dad about the benefits of having an outboard motor for the rowboat. He was positively alight with excitement at the possibilities. I'm told that I was a little bit of a budding Gloria Allred, myself, in my support of Mike's case, and Dad finally relented after thoroughly questioning our case.

For once, it was me in support of Mike, instead of the usual dynamic between us. Mike always seemed to relish being my big brother. He was quite good at it too. In my memory, he was always my champion, a good defender and protector. He mostly thought of me as his responsibility and it was him and me against the world, even when it came to our parents.

Mike took the fall for me on more than one occasion. Of course, the other side of that coin is that he was also my torturer and primary antagonist. He knew where all my buttons were and could easily access any one of them within the time it takes to burp or fart; two things that Mike also truly enjoyed doing. He was so proud of his ability to burp on demand.

Once we had that old Johnson mounted to the rowboat it didn't take us long to figure out that we didn't have to swim out to the raft anymore, if we didn't feel like it. We could motor down the canal, around the boat launch, right into the lake. The parameters of our ability to explore expanded far beyond what we could ever do with those oars. It seemed limitless to us. Of course, there were some rules for boating. The Adults had to know when we were taking it out and when we were to bring it back, and life jackets had to be worn at all times.

Along Anchor Bay Drive all of us kids had B-B Guns. Carl's was a pistol. Mike and I had matching pump action Daisy Rifles ge got as Christmas presents. Ammo was no problem. The Bait Store was always well stocked with tubes of B-Bs we could get for pennies. In the summer months, kids on Anchor Bay Drive would seldom be out and about without their trusty B-B Gun. There were lots of vermin around to maraud, frogs, toads, snakes, birds, mice and on and on.

One of the things that Mike, and I bonded over was frog hunting. In hindsight it surprises me how callous I was about these little murders; possibly because of the pay-off. Fried Frog Legs! I LOVED them, and no, they don't taste like chicken.

Mike was like a worker on a mass production assembly line about cooking them for us. He'd cut the frogs in half and skin their legs and pop them into a pan to cook. I always found it fascinating that the legs would start kicking when he plopped them into the hot grease. They would jump around in the pan for what seemed like ever, as if they were trying to jump out. Our only restriction was Dad and Shirley. They were our grease and seasoning dealers. One or both of them had to be nearby or we couldn't cook the frog legs.

Evidently, I had my own strategies for getting back at Mike for all his antagonism. One day, while he was messing with me about something, I looked down and realized I had my Daisy in my hand. I made it clear that if he didn't let up on me that he'd be sorry. He found this funny because he turned around laughing and running to get away from me. I shot him in what I was hoping would be the back of his head. It turned out that I'm not that good of a shot, because I got him in the ball of one of his hands as he ran.

It wasn't much of an injury. He ended up with a B-B sized dark purple dot on his palm. I will never forget the look of shock and astonishment on his face when he realized that I had actually shot him. All the jovial fun and games came to a screeching halt. He promptly walked over to me and grabbed my rifle and headed for the house.

The ensuing and ongoing education Dad and Mike gave me about gun safety has lasted to this day. I don't even own a gun and likely never will. They kept at me until they were sure I understood that you never point a gun at anyone! Ever!

Even at 7, Mike was well versed in hunting, fishing and camping and all that goes with it. He had an innate respect for all of it. Dad eventually did relent and gave me back my rifle, but only when he had convinced himself that I wouldn't do anything like that again, and he was right. I never did! Partly because of the love and admiration I had for my big brother and partly because I didn't want to be that kid.

To this day, I can't believe I shot my brother. It's an example of what I mean when I say that I was already beginning to act out over my family disintegrating before my eyes and I was helpless to do anything about it. What could I possibly have been thinking? I wasn't! That's the point, I was acting out.

There was a tree just beyond the patio in our back yard. Mike and I were both expert at climbing it, to the horror of Shirley and our dad. It was one of those things that Mike and I had to conspire about. "They just didn't understand us kids", we thought. "Kids climb trees, and we were kids". We had to be clandestine about it because we knew what the response would be if we were ever caught. I probably should have listened to the adults about it because there was one day when my climbing skills had abandoned me, if I ever had any to begin with. I think I may have gotten cocky about my abilities.

I was a ways up in that tree when Mike started getting nervous watching me from the ground. He had seen me climb that tree many times, often along with him. But today was different. He was nervous watching me this time. He was yelling at me to come down. He insisted that I was going too far. This was another of the few incidents in my life when

I have no explanation for my poor decision-making. I took it as a challenge to go further and so I did. To both of our surprise, I lost my footing and tumbled down the tree, hitting at least 2 branches on my way down. The sight must have been frightening. The fall certainly was.

Mike ran to get Dad, thinking I was dead. I had been knocked out for a minute and was quite dazed, but conscious, by the time Dad got to the scene. Mike was standing off to the side at the point of tears watching us as Dad examined me.

Both were sure I had broken at least one bone. As it turns out, I wouldn't break a bone until much later in my life. I was sore and shook, to be sure, but otherwise basically fine, which was confirmed by a doctor later that day. I may have had a concussion, but I wouldn't have known. I'm not sure if the field of medicine was even aware of what a concussion was in the 50s.

Whippings were few and far between on Anchor Bay Drive and always for the standard stuff that kids do. Willow tree branches were the favored weapons at such times. Weeping Willow trees were in abundance where we lived. Strip the leaves off a branch and you have an effective whip. Both Mike and I have felt that sting more than once while we lived there, sometimes even at one an other's hand.

One of those whippings was at Shirley's hand. It was well deserved and served up with passion and one of Dad's leather belts. Shirley was beside herself when she learned that Carl and I had broken into the Williamson's boat house. We had broken a window to get in. Evidently someone had seen it and alerted the Willimsons, who were in Detroit at the time.

They had a beautiful Cabin Cruiser up on straps in their boathouse. Carl and I, in a trance of criminality had broken into the boathouse and climbed into the boat. We were smoking the Parliaments and drinking the liquor that we found in the cabin. It wasn't like we got drunk or anything, but we did drink some of it. We thought we had gotten away with it because it wasn't until the next evening after dinner that I found out that Shirley had fielded a call from one of the Williamsons.

***

I've been dragged into criminal behavior a couple times in my life by people I liked a lot, and there actually is a kind of excitement that comes with trying to get away with committing an act that you know is a crime. It's nothing I'd ever gotten into very much, though, because along with the associated excitement, you also have to contend with consequences and the realization of what you are doing to other people. Committing a crime is something I would never think to do on my own. The only times I had ever committed a crime, it was in partnership with someone who talked me into it. I make no apology for being a creature of comfort. I don't want to deal with the residuals of being a criminal. That kind of excitement is just going to have to be left to other people; people like Carl Benocci, perhaps.

***

Shirley, having just learned about our crime from the phone call was livid and came bursting into the patio where Mike and I slept. She was spitting language the likes of which you would rarely hear outside of a Rap album with a parental advisory sticker prominently displayed on the cover. She proceeded to thrash me soundly before being interrupted by my dad. He was not particularly enthralled that she was doing *his* job and he told her about it right in front of me and a now frightened and cowering Mike.

Dad, as I mentioned, was a big guy as adults go, but I had never heard him bellow like he did at Shirley. Mike and I may have been witnessing the beginning of the eventual end of their marriage at that very moment.

I got off easy because Dad was so mad at Shirley. Their heated conversation moved to the kitchen while Mike and I tried to compose ourselves after the explosion of Shirley's rage. She wasn't happy about us being there to begin with, and now this? This wouldn't be my last transgression either.

Carl and I, playing over at his house one afternoon, stumbled onto a cache of his mom's shoes. Her feet were small enough that her shoes almost fit Carl and me. A couple of crumpled up pieces of newspaper packed into the toes of her shoes, and we were both good to go.

When I say, "Good to Go" I mean that we left the house in her shoes and went exploring, through brush and wet, marshy terrain. Well, I was exploring. Carl, it appears, was well versed and prepared for where we were going. We ended up in a tree where Carl, or more likely an adult, had built a little makeshift tree house.

The tree wasn't as perilous as the tree in our back yard. It grew at an angle, so we weren't all that high off the ground. Carl had talked me into getting naked with him. Being naked in the presence of another boy was nothing new to me. My Brother and I had often taken baths together and he was part of my education about how to pee-pee in the toilet. We used to have sword fights with our streams and thought it entertaining.

I had to admit, though, it felt good to be naked out in nature. I knew I wasn't supposed to do that, but what our parents didn't know wouldn't hurt them. Here we are, 2 little kids, wearing high heels and nothing else, climbing up a big tree. Fortunately, we were not within eyesight of anyone as far as we could tell. It was a marshy out of the way place near the lake. It wasn't about sex, of course. We were 5 for crying out loud. What did we know of sex? It was about acting up and doing stuff we knew we weren't supposed to.

On our way up to the tree house, Carl plucked a little twig off the tree and stuck it up his butt. I thought it weird, but not unlike the kind of weird that I had come to expect of him. What was unexpected was his skill at talking me into doing it as well. It took him a while to convince me to do it, but I finally did. I must admit, he was right. Once I got over the strangeness of what I was doing, it felt kind of nice.

I recall that we spent what seemed like quite a while up in that tree just hanging out, feeling the nature on our naked little bodies and talking about nothing, but it was a perfectly pleasant afternoon. Finally, we climbed back down the tree, put on our clothes and returned to Carl's house.

As we approached his house, there stood his mom at the back door with her hands on her hips and a somewhat menacing look on her face. As we approached, she could see our,,, well,,, *her* muddy, wet pumps and was not the least bit amused by it. She took a solid pinch on one of Carl's ears and dragged him into the back entryway, yelling at him as she did. I followed, because I needed to leave her shoes there and collect my own. I couldn't get out of there quickly enough even though her anger was not directed at me, right then. That anger would likely have been reserved for the next phone call that she would make to our house.

Dad was less than pleased, but mostly uncomfortable over the fact that I had been wearing *women's* shoes. I had never been Les' favorite. I made him uncomfortable in general. I don't recall him ever hugging me or playing with me unless he was drunk, and Mike was also involved. I'm reasonably sure that it was because of my effeminate demeanor. He and my brother were very close though.

I think Dad knew that this indiscretion didn't rise to a level requiring a willow switch. He just looked at me with an uncomfortable disapproval for a while and that was the extent of my punishment. Fortunately for me, Shirley wasn't about to lay into me with a switch either, she hadn't forgotten Dad's response the last time she did that. It wasn't long after that that it was decided that I would be going to live with Aunt Jo and Uncle Bill and our cousins in Mount Clemens. Mike would stay with Dad and Shirley.

CHAPTER 6

The House in Mt. Clemens

The house in Mt. Clemens looked like a mobile home with a thyroid condition, on the outside. Once inside, though, it was a log cabin in every respect. Even the detailing was rustic. There was an old west wagon wheel suspended sideways from the living room ceiling with a ring of lights along the outside hoop. There was a small shelf near the ceiling that circled the living room and displayed various riding tackle. It was like suddenly entering another whole world. The old west. It reminded me a lot of Earl's Cabin up North, only bigger.

I was staying with my Aunt Jo & Uncle Bill and my cousins. Uncle Bill was not happy with Dad and made no secret of it. He felt that Dad had abandoned his responsibilities as a father. It was only Uncle Bill's sense of duty that he learned in the Navy that kept me in the family.

Uncle Bill filed a petition in Family Court accusing Dad of abandonment. What I didn't know at the time was that mom had already made it clear to the rest of the family that she was with Paul now and he already had kids of his own and didn't want to take on any more.

Neither Mom nor Dad wanted me and living with Uncle Bill & Aunt Jo didn't feel at all secure. As much as I longed for my family to heal and for things to return to normal, it was not going to happen, and I was more of a problem to be solved than an actual member of the Schroeder Family. I couldn't conceptualize it at the time, but I felt it to my core. I really was alone in the world. After living at the house in Mt. Clemens, I would never live in a Schroeder household again.

I got the feeling that this was a bit of a lean period for Aunt Jo & Uncle Bill. There was no boat, and for the first time that I could remember, no new car. My dad and Uncle Bill bought new cars every year, each one trying their best to outdo the other. This year, Uncle Bill sold, or maybe lost, the big Pontiac station wagon and ended up with this big old bubble of a Chevy sedan that didn't really have a color. It seemed like it may have been light green at one time, but that was long ago.

Shortly after bringing this monstrosity home, Uncle Bill pulled it up into the garage and promptly took out a paint brush and began painting it red. We thought it strange for a car not to have a beautiful deep luster because that was all we had ever known. This old car now had a rough finish replete with brush hairs, brush strokes and specks of dust. Uncle Bill was oblivious to our chiding. He was already developing into the dedicated alcoholic he eventually became. He just kept painting that car and drinking his beer.

I remember that the refrigerator was locked with a big heavy chain. We ate well, but there was no freedom to raid the fridge for snacks anytime we wanted to like in the good old days. I think we were all aware for the first time in our young lives, what it meant not to be able to afford something. For me, it all came crashing down while getting ready for the school talent night.

Each of us in the class at Monteith Elementary was assigned the homework of writing a poem about the month of March. We were to recite our poems at a talent night in front of an audience of our families and friends. We were instructed that we all had to wear a green outfit and this specific shiny green St Patrick's Day hat made of cardboard with a layer of green foil. I had no green outfit and I guess there was no money for the hat. For some reason, the realization that I would not be able to be in the talent night with the others because we couldn't afford it, hit me really hard.

I went into a major crying jag. I was unsure for the first time in my life that things would ever return to normal. For Christ's sake, what even was "Normal" anyway? The incident seemed to trigger feelings of loneliness and fear about being apart from my Mom & Dad. I began to consider the possibility that they would never get back together. Feelings like I had no real home, and the one I was living in didn't seem all that secure, just then.

I was in the bedroom that I shared with my cousin Kathy. I was draped dramatically across the lower bunk crying hysterically when Kathy came in and in her usual confidently thoughtful way, said comforting things to try to get me to stop crying. "I have a pair of bright red pants we can put on you so you'll stand out and everybody will notice you" she said. "You'll be the only one with special red pants!" "Besides", she continued, "your poem is so good that no one will even notice that you don't have green clothes on."

I would not be consoled, not even by Kathy. She was my best friend and confidant. She could somehow sense that what I was crying about was a lot more than just some green clothes. She finally gave up and went looking for Aunt Jo to tell her what was going on.

I always got the feeling from Kathy that she understood what it was like to be unwanted by your parents like Mike and me. She was adopted too, but Aunt Jo & Uncle Bill stayed together and cared for and loved her and her brothers well.

Perhaps I shouldn't say, "Well". This family had their problems too. Kathy was essentially saddled with raising her, then 4 brothers. Another 2 brothers and a sister would be added later. Aunt Jo would go on to contract TB and diabetes and be essentially absent for a while, while Uncle Bill was struggling with alcohol and how to provide for a growing family. Being the oldest, Kathy was the one left standing to shepherd the family.

After a while, Aunt Jo came walking in with Kathy on her heels. She came into the room as Kathy leaned quietly against the door jamb. Aunt Jo sat on the floor across the bed from me. As was her style, she began mimicking my crying in that dramatic overacted way she was so good at. Aunt Jo was often a skilled parent and ordinarily this little act is so funny to watch, that we'd forget what we were crying about and bust out laughing. Once she got us laughing it was a piece of cake to get our young minds redirected to some other distraction. It was her superpower, her Magic!

When her trick would not do what it usually did, Aunt Jo realized as Kathy had, that this was about more than a talent show outfit. She sent Kathy out and closed the door behind her. Looking intently at me, she resumed her position on the floor across from me. She got quiet and serious and tried to get me to talk about what was really bothering me.

She eventually got me to talk about everything that was happening with Mom & Dad and Shirley and the separation and not being wanted and Uncle Bill being mad at my dad, and it made me cry even more. I was able to get across that I felt so alone in the world; how bad it felt, and how helpless I was to do anything about any of it.

I filled the room with pent up emotions that came rushing out like a flood. Poor Aunt Jo, It really seemed like she wanted to make it all better. She was so good at that but knew that this time she couldn't. She held me for a while and talked to me about life, and what was happening to me. I don't recall what she said, but I felt safe and loved for a moment. And maybe just for that moment, that's all I needed.

As the story about the talent show turned out, Aunt Jo somehow materialized a pair of green pants that sort of fit. I had a Madras shirt that had a lot of green in it. After talking on the phone with my Aunt Jo a few days before the show, my teacher decided that it would be green enough. We had found a big piece of green construction paper, or maybe card stock left over from some project. With some scissors and tape, we were able to fashion a hat that was shaped like it was supposed to, but there wasn't enough paper to make a top for it. So, we didn't. When I took a bow after reading my poem just like we had rehearsed, you could see the top of my head. That seemed to delight the audience and I thought it was cool that something I did got a laugh from a whole room full of people. It made up for how out of place I felt being dressed differently than the others. I remember the poem:

"March, March is so fair

March winds are everywhere

Watching kites up in the sky

Makes me wish that I could fly"

***

I got in major trouble with Uncle Bill one late autumn day while staying at the house in Mt Clemens. My cousin Danny and I were left to our own devices while everyone else was busy with something. We had long since been admonished not to play on the small bridge that connected our house to the rest of Michigan. We weren't supposed to be playing there because of the creek under the bridge. There were also no handrails to prevent little guys like us from falling in. Of course, being two years older than Danny, I wasn't a kid anymore and I was plenty old enough to play on the bridge like any other responsible adult.

I was able to entice Danny to cross the bridge with me, but he was visibly nervous about it because he knew neither of us were supposed to be there. It became too much for Danny when I began to climb down the embankment on the far side of the bridge. He was well aware that we were not allowed to play in the creek without an adult being there with us.

Why I was in such a rebellious, maybe even defiant, mood that day, escapes me. It was never like me to intentionally do things I had been specifically told not to do, let alone recruiting someone else into my dastardly deeds. I was a good little Catholic boy and good little Catholic Boys, don't do such things. Today was somehow different.

Against Danny's urgent warnings of impending doom, I brazenly climbed down to the creek and under the bridge. I was now out of Danny's sight line and decided to play it up by describing how cool it was down here and how much he was missing by being so scared. He was undeterred in his insistence that I come back up to the road, "Right Now!" So certain that I would be in the deepest of do-do for the rest of my natural life.

"You could fall in and drown", he called out, "Then what would happen?" "What an idea", I thought. I looked above me and reached for one of the support girders and realized that I could hang there and my feet would just barely touch the water. At this time of year, the creek wasn't quite a foot deep. I'll splash my feet around in the water and make Danny think I fell in. I started kicking my feet in the creek making as much noise as I could and started hollering for Danny to come down and save me.

Danny, not being able to see me, assumed that I really was in trouble and ran screaming over the bridge and down the driveway to the house. Here I am under the bridge still making all this noise and having the time of my life when suddenly, it hits me. I'm not really drowning, and Danny has just gone for help thinking that I am.

In about two minutes somebody, probably an adult, is going to come running down this road, fully expecting to find me floundering around in the creek, fighting for my life. "Oh shit. What am I going to do now?" I thought. I gave a moment's consideration to jumping in the creek to make my ruse look real, but it was cold out and I had no desire to find out just how cold the water was. I resigned myself to the reality that I was in trouble and the trouble I was in was much deeper than the creek.

I begin to climb back up to the road with my tail tucked between my legs. Just as I do, here comes Uncle Bill, running full bore with a frenzied look on his face with my cousin Danny, still screaming, in tow. When he sees me and it begins to register that I'm not dripping wet from head to toe, his expression changes almost instantly.

He is no longer the concerned parent come to rescue his little charge from the jaws of death, he is now an angry parent hell bent on kicking some butt. "You mean to tell me you're not drowning?" he yells from across the bridge. "What in the Sam Hill are you doing scaring the hell out of us like that?" He is still heading toward me, but he is no longer running. He is walking forcefully with a very definite stride almost as if he were marching. "Boy, when I get my hands on you, you're going to wish you were drowning!"

As he said that, he had finally reached where I was standing. He grabbed me by the arm, almost lifting me off the ground, and started dragging me back in the direction of the house. It seemed that with each step he took, he became angrier. By the time we got to the opposite end of the bridge he could no longer contain himself and started kicking me in the fanny to punctuate each word in what had now become a tirade of language that I'm certain I was too young to hear.

I wasn't paying attention to what he was saying. I was too overwhelmed by the intensity of his anger and his boat-shod foot kicking me in the backside. I'm pretty sure he wasn't really hurting me, but inside, I was a jumble of powerful emotions. I wanted to laugh and cry all at once. I was imagining what this whole scene must have looked like. Here was Uncle Bill, holding me out with this arm, kicking me in the butt and me flopping around with my arms and legs flailing in all directions like a rag doll. It somehow seemed funny to me, even while it was happening. At the same time, Uncle Bill's anger was very real, and it was directed at me.

What a casual observer might have heard me saying, wasn't so much "words" as it would have been incoherent blubbering punctuated by crying. Finally, Uncle Bill let go of my arm and with one last kick, sent me running for the house, yelling behind me to, "Get in that house and I don't want to see you coming out of that room until I tell you." The evidence would suggest that he eventually did tell me to come out of my room because I'm still here to tell you about it.

***

Not long after that, the court date for the neglect petition that Uncle Bill had filed against my dad had come. Uncle Bill loaded me up into the big red Chevy and headed to St Clair County Family Court. My Brother was already there as Uncle Bill dropped me off. I'm sure he was under the impression that his part in this family drama was concluded, and his brother would take it from there. He wanted no more part in it.

Mike was now 8 and I was 6. He and I were sitting on a bench just outside the courtroom. I knew that there was something big going on in there and my life was about to undergo a major change, again. I was scared to death about what that might end up being.

I suspect Mike knew what was happening on the other side of that big oak door because the whole time we sat on that bench he was holding me and promising me over and over that I was going to be OK. Finally, my brother and I were ushered into the courtroom. Dad and Shirley were at one table and Mom and Paul were at another. We had to stand there and listen while the people we knew as our parents both made their cases about why they didn't want to keep either one of us. Mike and I were remanded to the custody of St. Clair County, and I wouldn't see my brother again until after I graduated from high school. What I knew of as my family had just been scattered to the winds.

CHAPTER 7

Macomb County Youth Home.

Out of this whole family of Schroeders that I had been adopted into only a few years before; Grandma Schroeder in the Cabin up north, Grandma Lucille on Mom's side, Mom and her new husband, Dad and his new wife, Uncle Bill & Aunt Jo, all of them were done with me. By that time, I had developed some pretty tenacious low self-esteem, from these experiences, that follows me to this day. I was also saddled with having "Behavior Problems", the sum of which was that I was "effeminate" and "genteel". In all honesty, I guess my breaking into the Williamson's boat house didn't help much, even though it was handled quietly.

I don't know why I was being taken to a juvenile detention center. The only time I had ever seen the inside of a court room was earlier that day as my brother and I watched our parents tell the judge that they didn't want us anymore. I had never been arrested and I don't recall ever being told that I had done anything that would be considered a crime. The only thing I can think of is that there wasn't anywhere else for the court to put me, just then.

As I'm being turned over to the matrons at the Macomb County Youth Home, my consolation prize is a good-sized box of ribbon candy my Uncle Bill had given me. Along with that, I had a suitcase containing my entire life up to that point. The candy, by the way, was really nice. Brightly colored like the hard candy you'd expect to get at Christmas time. It was three long strips of candy scrunched up into zigzag shapes nestled next to each other. To eat it you would have to break a piece off one of the long strips.

I think I may be stuck on the memory of that box of candy because it was so good and looked so bright and festive. At that moment I really needed something truly pleasant to distract me from what was otherwise a thoroughly disintegrated life. Clearly, this candy was made to delight the senses. I really did want to enjoy it. If for no other reason than because it had become my only connection to a past, I somehow knew I would never see again!

I was ushered through several gray hallways and chambers separated by big heavy locked metal doors like you would see in any prison. The matron escorting me made sure to carefully lock each door we went through before opening the next one. My belongings, including my box of Ribbon Candy were immediately taken and put in a cage where the staff works.

There I was, banished to a world that had no connection to anything I knew yesterday sealed by the sound of a big heavy metal door closing behind me. That door was being locked and I thought about that as I cried myself to sleep that night. At the time, I didn't know what a metaphor was, but in hindsight, I had experienced one earlier that day.

This is actually a prison, so the decor is sparse, and all the tables and chairs are made of metal and they're bolted to the floor. I was given a pair of flip flops and a gray uniform that looked a lot like medical scrubs and issued a cell next to another boy who was already living there. He gave me the impression that he had been there for a while, and he was the one who taught me everything I needed to know about how things worked in this strange new place.

Everything was rigidly controlled. Mealtimes, play times, schooling, bed time and lights out all happened at the same time every day like clockwork. I never liked being in an environment where games, books and other stuff kids would normally need to occupy themselves were always under lock and key and you'd have to beg a staff person for access. Sometimes, if a staff person didn't like you or felt that you didn't behave well enough that day, permission would be denied. I've lived in such places a lot growing up.

There weren't many of us on this block. Maybe 5 or 6 but there was room for plenty more. After all, there weren't really all that many little kids my age that were already hardened and dangerous criminals in Michigan.

There were other cell blocks in this detention center where the older kids were housed. We could sometimes hear them, but we never actually saw them. I wasn't to be there for long. It was a stop on the way to another placement. I was only there for a few months. Just long enough to begin to adapt to the prison lifestyle.

There were only 2 highlights to my time in Juvenile lock-up. My house mate, let's call him "Eddie", because I can't recall what his name might have been, taught me how to self-asphyxiate. He taught me how to strangle myself. Of course, there was danger involved, but once you get to the point where you begin to pass out, your hands will naturally release their grip. I tried it once, at his direction, and found it a mildly interesting diversion, but never developed an interest in it like Eddie did. He seemed disappointed when I wasn't as excited about it as he was. I suspect I was Eddie's only friend at MCYH.

Eddie was obviously mentally ill. I was a weird kid and I had known my share of weird kids along the way, as you might imagine. I would go on to live, shoulder to shoulder among damaged and unwanted kids. Among that group, I was kind of in the middle. I did better than some and not as good as others.

In every group environment I've ever lived in, I have seen kids

I knew, classmates, get carted off to mental institutions or Juvenile Detention. Those were the kids I think I did better than. Most kids seemed well adjusted, compared to me, and seemed to be happy and productive. The cool kids, you might say. Those are the kids that I think did better than me.

But Eddie was in another category altogether. He brought a whole new level to the concept of the kind of weirdness that I was beginning to grow accustomed to. I just didn't have a reference point at that time to call it what it was; Mental Illness.

Eddie was in a total care environment for good reason. He was damaged in a way that messed him up *really* good. He was the type of kid who *would* cause harm to himself, albeit accidentally, with that self-asphyxiating stuff he was doing in the Bathroom. That was too weird, even for a damaged kid like me.

The other highlight at MCYH was my run in with the police. Me and Eddie spent a lot of our play yard time digging a hole under the fence as prisoners are want to do to. We did other things too, mind you. Like Eddie could do a standing forward flip. He would stand still and just jump into a flip and land on his feet like it never even happened. It was a sight to see. I tried to get him to teach me how to do it because I was so fascinated by it. Try as I might, I could never do it, despite his coaching. I gave up, one time, when I came straight down hard on the dirt right on my head, like a pile driver. I decided that that would be an experience I would have to leave to Eddie along with his self-asphyxiation. I could, however, do a relatively passable cartwheel. That was the first phase of Eddie's coaching on how to do a flip.

***

We finally did get out through our hole under the fence and got as far as about halfway through a crop field that bordered one side of the play yard, before being nabbed. Two squad cars with sirens blasting and lights flashing had responded almost immediately. They pulled up on a road that bordered the opposite side of the crop field we were trying to get through. One of the matrons must have seen us breaking out. It was almost like the police were waiting for us. It was that fast. They didn't have to go far to book us, either. The Detention Center couldn't have been more than a football field away.

When I think about it today, there's no way that the matrons didn't know what me and Eddies were up to. It took us days to dig that hole and when we were called back into the detention center after play time we covered it up with a piece of cardboard. Granted, it wasn't that big of a hole. We weren't that big. But the matrons couldn't possibly have been that clueless. They had to know. Perhaps that's why the police were so quick to catch us. The matrons must have alerted them to expect it before it even happened.

I would go on to run away once from every institution/group living situation I would ever live in. It was always because of fear or frustration with what was happening where I lived. Home is supposed to be where you go to get away from violence or other mistreatment. But what are you supposed to do when what you feel a need to get away from is happening right there in your living space?

I wouldn't end up doing well in normal family settings either. I didn't fit in and appearing to be gay was central to most of the problems I encountered growing up. That, and being a standard issue hard-headed Taurus was the cross I had to bear. It was shortly after my big jailbreak from MCYH that I was moved to Mrs. Rae's Children's Home.

CHAPTER 8

Mrs. Rae's Children's Home

I would find myself at Mrs. Rae's Children's Home in Port Huron, three times in my young life. It was kind of like a second home in the sense that it was where I'd be taken between failed foster placements. I associate Mrs. Rae's with two things, cars and prison. Picturing where I was will be helpful. There was a huge, fenced yard that wrapped halfway around a beautiful old two and a half story brick mansion beyond which was a huge vegetable garden. Our play yard was big enough to entertain about 15 or 16 youth ranging in age from about 5 to 17.

There was a swing set and jungle gym that was well made from the hardiest metals; the kind that could surely cause burns on a hot summer day and easily strong enough to ward off a military tank assault. Off to the far corner of the yard was a baseball diamond that was seldom used for baseball. It was too close to Mrs. Rae's apartment windows; the few windows in the whole building that didn't have bars on them. Apparently, nobody seemed all that concerned that Mrs. Rae might want to mount a jailbreak.

There was an above ground pool just outside the fence that they put up for us every summer. We had a section of the basement where sporting equipment would be stored, laundry would be done and it was also our dressing room for those days when we could enjoy the pool; separately from the girls of course. We had to play in the pool in shifts.

It was in that basement that I learned that I had a little dick because dick size was a frequent subject of discussion in boy's locker rooms. The older boys, of course, were somewhat bigger by nature and were more likely to display themselves while changing. I was pretty rigidly modest and it took a bit of threatening from the others to get me to reveal. Once I did, I was instantly sorry I had. As if my housemates didn't already have enough ammunition, now I had a reputation for having a little dick and it took me being sent off to another foster placement to make it stop.

***

The second floor was our bedrooms. Well, our cells, actually. There were three or four of us to a cell, depending on the size of the room. There were cells on both sides of a long hallway and another on each end. The hallway was broken up by the Bathroom on one side and a storage closet on the other. That closet is where the shoes that turned my toes into infected goo came from, during one of my incarcerations there. More on that later.

My room was on one end of the hallway near the stairway for a while and later at the other end. This is where prison comes into play. Each cell had big heavy doors with a small square window in it and the other widows in the rooms all had bars on them. The doors were always locked when we were upstairs. Probably to keep the girls and boys separated as well as preventing us from running away. Everybody wanted to run away, but few at Mrs. Rae's ever did during the times I lived there. We were mostly boys, but there were some girls too. Possibly relatives like Sarah and Gary Tucker.

I loved cars! From actual automobiles, all the way down to those little Matchbox Cars, my mom used to placate me with, back home. I had quite the collection. I still had a few, along with a Ford Starliner model that I had built myself. Outside, there on the baseball diamond I would build roads, parking lots, bridges, tunnels and the like and let my imagination run wild building a story to involve my little cars in. That would keep me out of other trouble for hours on end.

By this time, I had almost grown to expect to be bullied on a playground and often the other kids would destroy my little diasporas, but I never learned to shake it off when they did. It bothered me because I couldn't understand why someone would come along and destroy someone else's joy like that, just because they could. But then, that's not how I responded to trauma. I wouldn't do that to anyone because I was well versed on what it feels like to be on the receiving end of such senseless cruelty. Sometimes hurt people, hurt people because it's all they know. Me and my little cities, carved into the baseball diamond, were an easy target because I obviously wasn't the type to fight back.

I could tell you the make, model and year of just about any car on the road, at the time. Cars used to look distinctly different from one another back then. There were identifiable style elements that each brand had that set them apart from the others. It wouldn't be until years later that automakers would begin falling all over each other trying to resemble one aother's designs.

I would beg Brooksie or Bessie for magazines and would occupy myself cutting the pictures of the cars out of them and sliding the little pictures around on the floor making engine noises until lights out. My interest in cars had nothing to do with what made then run. My romance was with the designs. They were presented with true glamour. The pictures of cars in magazines were mostly airbrushed works of art. Automakers sure knew how to market cars to little gay kids; or maybe it was just me.

On the first floor was our playroom, a dining room, a large parlor, the kitchen and Mrs. Rae's apartment. Mrs. Rae's apartment was the mystery wing of the mansion. None of us had ever seen the inside of it beyond what you could see when Mrs.

Rae would fling the door open to complain about the noise we were making in the playroom.

She was an old white-haired lady with no shortage of costume jewelry. If she had ever been married, her husband was long gone and she didn't appear to have any children of her own. She rarely left her wing of the mansion. When she did, it usually wasn't to interact with us. I imagine a rich old white lady had civic Port Huron matters to attend to. But who knows? She was essentially a hermit.

When new residents would arrive, they would come in the front door into the parlor for a bit and would never see the front door or the parlor again. It was off limits to us. We all entered the house from the play yard through the kitchen and dining room, to the playroom.

We weren't allowed to leave the playground but for school, church and working in the garden. The garden was the source of most of the food we ate. It was huge and bore us a wide range of things to eat when in season. Some of us would be called into service for planting, hoeing and weeding, as a redirection from deviations from proper decorum.

The third floor was kind of like a tower. There was nothing up there but two prison cells with 2 bunk beds in each and a small bathroom "Area". The cells were joined to the bedroom hallway by a flight of stairs. Next to that stairway was another longer one leading all the way down to Mrs. Rae's apartment.

The cells were side by side in what I'm sure was once one big day room before it was repurposed. Back then, a day room was where members of a well to do household would convalesce when they were sick. They would have lots of windows that could be open to let in sunshine and fresh air to help with recovery.

But these 2 cells were bordered on 3 sides with paned windows, all of which had bars on them to prevent escape. Each window had a brass crank that would swing the window open when needed. The cells overlooked the play yard. There would often be conversations between the kids in lock-up and the kids playing in the yard. The kids in lock-up would be badly in need of anything that would occupy the hours.

Our jailer was another old white woman named Mrs. Brooks, who lived in. She was very much a character like those that you'd see in old black & white movies. She was a short and stout bulldog of a woman that sounded and acted a lot like Jimmy Cagney. Her superpower was her kindness. She didn't use it all that much but when she did, it was clear that she knew the effects of trauma as well as any of us did. However, her resting pulse was more like a cranky bulldog. Most of us were broken children and a decided lack of tolerance was sometimes called for. We called her "Brooksie" and she was up to the task.

The day Gary Tucker and his little sister, Sarah, were brought in, Brooksie was leading them to the upstairs bathroom that I had just come out of, muttering under her breath what was probably a tirade of language that would make a drunk sailor proud.

Gary and Sarah had badly matted hair that was riddled with lice. It was Brooksie's job to dispense with the unwanted insects before they spread to the rest of us. She sprayed both heads with something and cut Gary's hair off. Well, it was more like shaved off. You could do that to little boys back then. Sarah was another story. Brooksie studiously combed the critters out of Sarah's hair as she washed and conditioned it to try to get most of the matting out. She did have to do a little bit of cutting, though, and the resulting coif was a testament that Brooksie was not much of a cosmetologist.

The arrival of new residents at Mrs. Rae's was often fraught with high drama. There was an energy to it that would briefly permeate the household as these broken children were being extricated against their will, kicking and screaming, from an even more harrowing environment. It wouldn't be long, though, before an uneasy calm would be restored as our new siblings would come to realize that, although they were clearly in a kind of jail they were, at the very least, safe for now.

Gary Tucker would go on to be my best friend at Mrs. Rae's. We were inseparable. He was a fountain of fun ideas and a master at games like "Let's Pretend". He would incorporate me, his little sister and sometimes Mary Christmas Day as actors in his wild and engaging tales of adventure. Mary Christmas Day was, as you might guess, born on Christmas and her family name, conveniently, happened to be "Day".

Mary was a retarded girl around our age and liked hanging out with us because we were a little family of kids who were routinely ridiculed and harassed by the others. She liked being told what do because it made her feel included, and the stories Gary would come up with were lots of fun to act out. Most of Gary's stories would be imagined right there, on the fly. Most were swashbuckling stories of danger and heroism, in which Gary, of course, would be the hero. What an imagination the boy had.

Sometimes he would hit the wall on a story and not know where to go with it. The rest of us could sense it and would chime in with an idea or two which would start him right up again. Gary Kept us busy for many hours out there in the yard. Others would often overhear us working on a story and laugh at us. Their laughter would roll off of us like water off a duck's back. We were having a good time in our heads with our little imaginings. Fully engaged, you might say. The fact that we were together in our imaginings made the jeering hurt less than it otherwise, would.

One of the things that has followed me through a lot of the places where I've lived is the curiosity boys have about how other boys fight. Particularly genteel or effeminate boys like me. I've never understood that, and it has happened to me several times in different group settings.

I'm a gay kid trying to make a way in the world, pretty much on my own. My behavior is clearly effeminate, which made me a target for harassment by most of the other kids regardless of where I lived. Gender roles were still quite rigidly enforced by peers and stewards alike in the 60s. I was likely the only one in my world who didn't know I was gay. People weren't allowed to be gay back then. At one time or another, I've been called each and every one of the veritable dictionary of terms alluding to homosexuality. My behavior seemed to trigger the straight boy's curiosity about how I fight. I abhor violence. It's OK for movies, but not for real life.

Being manipulated into a fight happened to Gary and me once. The older boys would get us apart and start filling our heads with animus against each other to get us to fight. The one time it actually did come to blows between us, it was in the yard. We swung wildly at one another like windmills and ended up wrestling around on the dusty baseball diamond. Neither of us knew what we were doing and didn't want to be in that situation to begin with. I can only imagine what we must have looked like while the others gathered around us, egging us on. The fact that I can't remember who won the fight would suggest that it was probably Gary.

We were, of course, brought up on charges by Bessie and Brooksie. Bessie was exactly what you would think she was. She was the embodiment of "Mammy" in "Gone with the Wind", chastising Scarlett O'Hara for flirting with so many gentlemen suitors and refusing to eat enough to keep herself from getting the vapors. Bessie was a woman to whom Food = Love. She was our Chef and clearly in charge of the house.

Gary and I were ordered to sit in those familiar dining room chairs and endure advanced education in gentlemanly decorum. As if that wasn't enough to focus our attention they brought in

Mrs. Rae to apply additional fear and trembling to cement the message of the Household's demand of appropriate behavior.

We got a pretty good earful about it, even though neither of us needed it. We didn't want to fight to begin with. It was our mutual bonding over licking our wounds and enduring the adults' lectures that brought us back together as friends. After that, we learned to shine the others on when they tried to set us against one another. We had learned what they were up to.

The social environment at Mrs. Rae's Children's home, and another reason it seemed like a prison, was that bad kids were almost lauded for being bad. The more serious the offense you had committed was like bigger, more noticeable notches on a Wild West gunslinger's belt. It was meant to instill respect, fear and reverence. The kind of offenses that would get you thrown into lock-up would be stuff like running away, skipping school, smoking, drinking, flipping out in an uncontrolled rage (which happened a *lot*), or maybe getting pregnant. It was mostly the older kids who got into that kind of trouble.

I did end up in Lock-Up once along with Gary. One day while out in the yard, playing "Let's Pretend" the story veered into the difference between boys and girls. Gary called me over to see Mary Christmas Day because he had just talked her into showing him her vagina. "Have you ever seen a pussy?" he half whispered through his excitement. "No" I truthfully replied. "Come here, you have got to see this!" He led me over to the corner of the yard by Mrs. Rae's bedroom window. It was the only place in the yard that wasn't within easy eyesight of one of the adults, with the possible exception of Mrs. Rae.

Once we were gathered in the corner, Mary pulled down her skirt and then her panties. She seemed almost proud of it as she smiled broadly like she had just baked a cake or something. I guess the encouragement she had gotten from Gary a few minutes ago was having her feeling pretty good about herself.

Gary, probably showing off for me, reached down and touched Mary's privates and encouraged me to do the same. I wasn't interested, but I did appreciate that I had seen an actual vagina. Of course, I had little interest in it beyond that.

I don't know this to be true, but Mrs. Rae must have seen at least some of what we were up to. It wasn't long after Mary had rearranged herself that Bessie came running out carrying a broom with a determined stride. Using her broom, Bessie swept us in the direction of the kitchen door. The three of us were brought up on charges and made to sit in the dining room again and think about what we had done. Brooksie, Mrs. Rae and Bessie were giving us the business about having sex. We hadn't actually gotten that far but they didn't seem to know that.

The three of us sat there in our guilt for some time as the adults went into the kitchen, no doubt to strategize what would happen next. Mary Christmas Day was ushered in first. After a while, Bessie opened the kitchen door and ceremoniously called me and Gary into the kitchen. Brooksie was still there. Both Mary and Mrs. Rae had left. Mrs. Rae's job of instilling fear and trembling had already been accomplished.

Bessie was scolding us while Brooksie chimed in every now and then. Perhaps Bessie didn't think we were paying close enough attention to what she was trying to get us to understand. She talked about how disgusting it was, the way we took advantage of a poor little retarded girl who didn't know any better. She stopped talking for a minute and breathed a heavy sigh. You know the one. The one where she's about to do something that was going to hurt *her* more than it would hurt *us*.

She reached for her trusty meat cleaver. "Ok, boys," she sighed. "Put those weenies right here on the cutting board." she immediately raised the cleaver indicating a willingness to cut our little dicks off and slammed the blade into the cutting board with a good amount of force. Gary and I began crying as she raised it again and motioned towards the cutting board. "Get 'em out, I'm gonna cut 'em off!", She insisted.

Gary and I, already trembling from Mrs. Rae's disdain, went into a panic. How either of us managed not to pee ourselves is beyond me, but we pleaded for our lives and promised never to do it again because Bessie had us believing she was really going to do it. Finally, Bessie motioned to Brooksie to take us to Lock-up. Brooksie dutifully grabbed each of us by an arm and angrily dragged us up the stairs to our fate, grumbling as she did.

Lock-up was terrible because there was absolutely nothing left to occupy us after getting acquainted with our ominous surroundings and discussing how much this was going to do for our street cred. It slowly became clear why we would often hear people in Lock-Up freaking out, causing a ruckus and otherwise trying to get Brooksie's attention in the middle of the night to beg for a magazine or book or playing cards or something. Or maybe try to fake a medical emergency to get out of that cell, even for just a moment. Suddenly, that second staircase to Mrs. Rae's apartment made all the sense in the world. She needed that so she could fling her door open and demand quiet up in the cells so she could get some sleep.

In lock-up we were truly in prison, day and night. Our meals were slid through a hole in the door and they weren't much. The expectation was that we would do nothing other than introspection about our misdeeds. That took us about 5 minutes. We knew we were wrong, and we got caught and brought up on charges for which we knew we were guilty. It really wasn't brain surgery to try to dissect and analyze. Lock-up never lasted for more than a couple days, but it felt like months because of the boredom.

***

At school, which was a little over a block away, we were almost famous just for being orphans from Mrs. Rae's Children's home.

Everybody knew. When you're a kid with a stormy history that brought you to a place like this, you were seen through a lens of pity. It felt like we were a strange curiosity whose very existence instilled a sense of wonder and sympathy.

Mrs. Miller was my teacher. She reminded me a little of the cartoon character Betty Boop. She was good looking and dressed the part. She clearly liked looking the way she did. She would slither around the classroom swaying those hips much like I did. She was admirably sensuous and had one thing I didn't. Confidence.

She sat me next to Betty McDermott, a black girl, who was also confident. She was pretty and friendly. I think she was my girlfriend, or at least she wanted to be. She treated me like we were a couple right from the start. I liked the attention, and we became fast buddies. She told me, one day, that she had pubic hair and wanted to show it to me after school. That never happened because I had already seen a vagina and knew I had no interest in it. I just didn't show up. She never brought it up after that.

Betty and I would always sit together, with some of her friends, at lunch and laugh and joke about everything. I had heard a dirty joke that I was sure she would love. I began to tell the story, but just as I got to the punch line, where I was supposed to say, "Well your purse is open and your lipstick is hanging out." one of the nuns approached, seemingly intent on hearing the punch line.

I wonder, now, whether she had already heard the joke and was waiting to pounce once the offending punch line was delivered. I had to think on my feet and came up with an alternate line that ended up not being funny, even to me. I have, at least, a reference point of what a comedian goes through when they bomb in a spectacular fashion. The silence hurt to the point where I felt almost physically wounded. But, the nun did nothing, and that was the point of veering off book. Out of a sense of shame, I don't think I ever finished telling Betty the actual joke.

***

Music education was still a thing in school. Everybody had to go to music class. Ours was as basic as it gets. There wasn't an actual classroom for music. We gathered in a repurposed garrison hut that stood away from the rest of the school building. Our teacher was a former military officer who reminded me of the character George Costanza on the sit-com "Seinfeld".

He had some old songbooks that he kept in a cupboard. He would pull them out and teach us to sing the songs. That was the extent of it. The class was absolutely for his own pleasure. He loved to sing, despite the fact that he wasn't very remarkable at it. He could sing, of course, but there wasn't anything remarkable about it other than he was obviously enjoying it. He seemed undeterred about that and almost like a coach; he would do his best to get us excited about it, sometimes successfully. "The Caissons Keep Rolling Along", "Surrey with the Fringe on Top", "My Wild Irish Rose", "The Yellow Rose of Texas". Songs like you'd hear a barbershop quartet sing. It passed the time, and Betty and I could sit together. Betty was a good singer, probably the best in our class.

Back at the home, we got a new kid who was probably 15 or 16 and the only place open at the time was in my cell. His name was Ernie, and he had a whopper of a dick that he was quite proud of. It was his conversation starter and he used it well. He was damaged and probably hated himself passionately like the rest of us. But he had this big dick that got him the attention and street cred he so desperately desired. It was what he had to work with, and in a situation like ours, you use what you have to get what you need.

He was standing and masturbating over by the window and watching for our reaction. Of course, we were fascinated. He was older than us so it never occurred to us that we could tell him to stop doing that because it was inappropriate. You just don't tell older kids what to do; they tell *you*!

He talked one of the other boys into jacking him off. It was fascinating to look at and he did get me to "Shake Hands" with it for a quick second. I *did* like that. It was the first time I had ever seen an erection and this one was freakishly large. I liked it, but not enough to go any further despite his encouragement.

Suddenly it was lights out. In the dark, I could hear him telling the other boy what to do and how to do it. He was instructing all of us how to masturbate. I tried to follow his instructions but it didn't make much sense to me. I was too young to understand why someone would do that. It was weird to me. While we were engrossed with playing with our dicks, the evidence would suggest that Brooksie must have seen or heard at least some of what was going on, because everything changed the next day. Gary and I got moved to the cell on the far end of the hallway and Ernie was ushered off to "Lock-Up".

As far as I could tell, Ernie never did come out of lock-up. Perhaps we weren't the only kids Ernie was stirring up with his prized possession. He was probably ushered off to some treatment facility to attempt some sort of rehabilitation. In my imagination, he would have gone on to be a professional sex freak of some kind. He was certainly built for it.

Gary and I ended up with a younger kid staying in the room at the other end of the hallway, near the stairway to the tower. I would spend my time with my magazines and the cars I cut out of them. Gary would read whatever was in the magazines I left after dissecting what I wanted, like how families on TV divide the Sunday Paper into the sections of individual interest and then pass the remaining sections around to the others.

I wanted to be anyone other than me. I wanted peace, I wanted fun. I wanted to be loved, I wanted to be with my family like it used to be when things weren't so awful. I just wanted anything but this! I didn't think I was particularly remarkable in any perceivable way. I didn't have something to work with like Ernie did, or Gary with his imagination. I needed something so badly and didn't feel like I had the tools to get it. So, I decided I wanted to be blind like Patty Duke in the movie about Helen Keller. Maybe that would get me what I wanted; whatever that may have been.

I wanted anything to distract me from how I felt inside. I had heard that if you stared at the sun, you'd go blind, so I decided to try it right there in our cell. I stared at the bare light bulb on the ceiling for a long time hoping that it would make me blind and change my life. It didn't, and I felt disappointed about that. Becoming someone else would have to wait for another day.

CHAPTER 9

The Macklems

The day I arrived at the Macklem's it was a beautiful summer day. The weather was nothing short of perfect. Mr. Fox drove us up a long unpaved driveway through a creek bed to a small 2 story farmhouse with weathered split rail fence. It may as well have been a scene from "Little House on the Prairie".

Mr. Fox and Mrs. Macklem talked for a few minutes as I walked idly over to the fence. Mrs. Macklem was a farm wife from head to toe. She wore a flowered one-piece, short sleeved dress, buttoned up to the neck. Over that, a blue plaid apron that showed little evidence of wear. She wasn't particularly old and carried herself with a polite dignity. Meanwhile, I was drawn to the fence by a few ponies grazing in the field just a few feet from me. They were lovely to look at and seemed idle and calm, like I did just then.

After a few minutes Mr. Fox called me over to report that it was time for him to return to Mt Clemens. He reminded me that I would be fine in the Macklem's care and said his goodbyes. I sadly watched as the only person in the world that I knew yesterday, slowly made his way down the long driveway and out of my sight. There I was again, feeling alone in the world.

This farm would be my introduction to hard labor and living with farm animals, like "Jellybean", for instance. Jellybean was a foal that had recently been rejected by his mother, as Mrs. Macklem explained. That's why there was a thoroughly average looking sandy colored pony walking up to me in the front yard, un-tethered. "Jellybean got kicked through that fence right over there a few weeks ago." she told me. The fence had since been repaired and Jellybean was so friendly that the Macklems decided to let him stay where he seemed to be happy.

As she spoke, Jellybean was gently bumping me in the arm with his head. "Notice me!" he seemed to be saying. Mrs. Macklem showed me what ponies want when they do that. She rubbed his head on the flat surface between his eyes, the side of his jaw and around his ears. She went on to pet him along his neck. She seemed to know what Jellybean wanted. "That's what happens sometimes." she said. "Sometimes an animal's mother will simply reject her offspring. Who knows why?"

She didn't seem to be happy or sad about it. It was more like she was simply reciting a natural fact. The irony was not lost on me. I was applying what she had just said, to my own life. She explained that Jellybean would be sold as soon as he was weaned. One of my many jobs would be feeding Jellybean from a big baby bottle that I would guess was made for big animals that might need a little help early on.

Mrs. Macklem went on; I had 3 Foster siblings who would be returning from school a little later today. Tony and Donna Domshaw were siblings who had already been fostered there, and Bonnie, the Macklem's own daughter. Tony and Mr. Macklem would begin my education in daily chores later that day.

In the Macklem household, the boys and girls were always separated. Bonnie and Donna shared a room and me and Tony shared another. Our rooms were separated by a landing and a staircase leading to the ground floor. Many a jocular Male v Female argument would take place across that little landing which would invariably stir a shout to pipe down, from Mr. or Mrs. Macklem from their bedroom just below us.

But that wasn't the only thing that separated the genders. Donna and Bonnie were in High School. They had to wait by the highway at the end of our long driveway, for a bus to take them to school, while Tony and I walked, or sometimes sledded, through a forest and up a punishing hill to an appropriately named one room schoolhouse. Pine Hill School it was called.

There have been 2 periods of my life when I had to walk great distances to and from a one room schoolhouse. My stay at the Macklem Farm was one of them. They were also the only 2 schools I attended that weren't Catholic.

Mr. Lentz was our teacher and grades 1 through 8 were all taught in one classroom. There were barely over a dozen of us, all from neighboring farms. I was in 3rd grade. The good and bad thing about Mr. Lentz having so few students was that he could call each farm individually to deliver report cards and evaluations. I would guess that Mr. & Mrs. Macklem liked the arrangement just fine, but it wasn't always such a good thing for me and Tony.

In Michigan at the time, kids were routinely fostered to rural families who would be paid a stipend every month by the State for our care. It was a good deal for the foster households. They would get some money for our support, along with free farm labor.

At the Macklem Farm, we were definitely put to work. Tony and I had to get up early every morning before school to milk and feed the cows. We did have mechanical help though. There was piping overhead throughout the barn to provide water for the Automatic watering bowls that each stall had. The cows would simply push the lever with their snout and the bowl would fill with water for them.

The rest of the overhead piping was for the vacuum system used to power the buckets with the 6 milking suction cups. All Tony and I would have to do is attach the bucket to the pipe and the cups to the cow's teats and wait a few minutes while gently rubbing their udders toward the suction cups. We only had one bucket, so Tony and I would switch off between milking, shoveling manure and laying down fresh straw. We would then take the bucket, now full of warm milk, to the separator and pour it in.

The separator would separate the cream from the milk and pasteurize it. The milk would then flow into big metal canisters. A truck would come by to pick them up and off to market they would go and be replaced by empty canisters for tomorrow's milk. Most days, Mrs. Macklem would come out to the barn while all of this was going on, to gather milk and cream for the house, some of which would be made into butter and cheese.

The barn and the procedures we did everyday were comforting to me. There was a predictable sameness about it that I liked. I developed relationships with the cows. I doubt that these cows were having any kind of relationship with me, though. I never got the impression that they cared one way or the other, what I did. I don't think cows have that capacity. I don't recall a cow ever walking up to me for attention or anything other than food, perhaps. I suppose they recognized that I was there and familiar to them, but not much beyond that.

Those cows and ponies, along with exploring the Macklem's 40 acres were the centerpiece of what joy I experienced while I lived there. Each of the stalls were labeled with the individual cow's name and I, most often, worked the aisle in front of the cows. That's where we would have mash waiting for them when we called them in to milk them. If I wasn't fast enough, occasionally one of them would lose interest in the stall and wander around the barn. That became another chore altogether. Moving a cow back to their stall once they were un-tethered added a whole new dimension to our normal chores.

Afterwards me, or Tony, would go behind the cows and pitch their manure out of a long cement trench, into a wheelbarrow and load it onto the spreader to be taken to the fields for fertilizer, or sold to neighboring farms for their fields. Then it was time to change clothes, have breakfast and head off to school.

After school, we would have to call in the cows in and settle them in the barn for more feeding and milking. "Kaboss, Kaboss", we would shout at the top of our lungs! I guess the cows knew what that meant, even though I never did. I asked, a few times, but no one seemed to have an explanation. That's just how it had always been done. That sound, whatever it means, would bring the cows running from whatever pasture they were grazing in at the time.

There were 7 cows and about as many Ponies at the farm. Shetland ponies, I learned, were the most desirable and commanded the best price. There were also a gaggle of chickens, for eggs and a piglet that Tony and I had been given in exchange for helping the other farmers bale and store hay and straw for the winter. His name was "Little Griz" after the farmer who gave him to us. All these animals needed some type of routine care every day and that was our job.

When we got "Little Griz", he was a young piglet. We didn't even have a pen for him. We built a trough for him and put up a single strand of electric wire in a square about the size of an average bedroom. Little Griz learned his parameters quickly and rarely pushed his trough out of its boundaries. He was a messy beast who would eat whatever was dumped in his trough. Usually, it would be table scraps from the house, chaff from the garden and sometimes some of the milk that had spoiled. As a piglet, Little Griz was dripping with a charming cuteness, but as he quickly grew, that cuteness slowly began to resemble a kind of selfish anger that was more along the lines of what pigs are generally like.

Once he was almost grown, Mr.Macklem smiled at us and instructed us to remove the fence entirely. We objected, but he insisted that the fence wasn't needed anymore. He was right!

Little Griz never left his now invisible pen, even at our chiding and cajoling. Once he was fattened up, he was butchered, right there in one of the barns. That was hard to watch, but the real Griz and Mr. Macklem were well acquainted with the process and didn't seem to mind it at all. It was business as usual, to them, which made it a bit less gruesome to me.

Out there in rural Michigan groups of Farms would co-op harvests by joining together and going from farm to farm to harvest whatever each farm was growing. One farmer might own a combine, another might have a hay baler, another some other big expensive piece of equipment. Each of those machines would be used on each of the farms while all of the various family members would become the labor force. The women would be cooking and serving for the whole group while taking over chore duties on each of the farms involved.

We could polish off one farm in a day, or maybe 2, and then move on the next one. The whole process took about a week and a half. To this day, it's the hardest I have ever worked. A bale of hay, you might consider, weighed about as much as I did, at the time. Even Donna and Bonnie were called into service. Donna, bless her heart, was out there with us in her cowboy boots and blue jeans, throwing bales of hay like it was nothing. She wasn't that big either. What she *did* have was heart and surprising strength. Bonnie cooked with the other women and handled our chores while we were at other farms.

After the harvest, everyone's barns would have hay-lofts packed full of bales of hay and straw. It didn't take Tony and me long to imagine tunnels, caves and forts we could build into that big pile of bales. It would appear that we weren't the first ones to think of it. Mr. Macklem gave us a handful of planks to use to prevent a ton of bales from coming crashing through our little caves and crushing us to death. He would grudgingly help with construction because he knew it was going to happen anyway and he wanted to make sure the ensuing tunnels and caves would be as safe as could be expected.

With what little free time we had, Tony and I were having no trouble finding things to occupy our attention. There were 40 acres, including 2 barns and plenty of old forgotten farming equipment to explore; and, of course, a stable full of Ponies to ride.

Another thing I loved about living on a farm was the smells. The smell of Hay and the smell of Straw are different. The smell of fresh, moist soil. The smell of the mash we fed the Cows was a combination of oats, wheat and corn ground up together. The smell of warm milk as we milked the cows. Even the smell of different animal's manure. Pony manure doesn't have much of a smell, but cow manure, as I'm sure you know, has a distinctive and pungent odor that wasn't altogether unpleasant to me. There is something about all these smells that felt earthy and comforting to me.

One of the antiques, often found on a farm, was a beautiful, ornate cutter that had clearly seen better days. Mr. Macklem bragged to us that he had gotten it for a song, some years ago, and was quite proud of himself. He set himself from time to time to restoring the old cutter and the resulting repairs brought the wreck back to its former glory. We all got to enjoy it for a while before Mr. Macklem had to sell it to buy more hay as the winter had lasted longer than expected. A lot of things on a farm must be carefully timed to seasons that are not always congruous. The finished cutter, however, was a thing of beauty that likely brought a pretty penny when it was sold.

A creek ran through the Macklem's land. It was relatively small most of the year and crossed the driveway. In the spring the creek would rise making it impassable by foot or vehicle. Tony and I helped Mr. Macklem build a short bridge out of what looked like railroad ties so that heavy vehicles could pass when needed. We also helped Mr. Macklem build a little shack for Bonnie and

Donna to wait in for the school bus during the snowy winters. It had a door from an old phone booth and a generator so they could have some heat in there while they waited. Winters in Michigan got pretty cold. The pay-off for helping Mr. Macklem with building things was that he showed us the spot on our land where the creek was deep enough to swim in but only in the spring and summer. He also taught us how to tap the maple trees so Mrs Macklem could make syrup for our pancakes.

One day, a man that I had never met before, showed up at the Macklem's. He was well dressed and handsome. He had the air of a man who was accustomed to having money. He had brought with him the biggest, oldest, most beautiful bicycle I had ever seen. It was a red & white Schwinn and had built-in headlights and taillights that worked. The cross bars were shiny, beautifully painted metal almost like a car. It had 2 big springs in front, attached to the body to smooth out the ride. It had the look of an antique that had been meticulously cared for.

The man spoke with Mrs. Macklem and me as he described the features of this wonderful machine and then handed it over to me. He and Mrs. Macklem watched me ride around among the barns for a while and then the man politely said his goodbyes. I never saw the man again after that. I was sad to have to leave that beautiful bike behind when I was returned to the Foster system. I was going somewhere where I couldn't take it. I have often wondered about that gift, the man who brought it to me, and how he knew of me.

Another wonderful thing about living on a farm is readily available ponies. Ours were mainly for breeding. They weren't beasts of burden at the farm with the occasional exception of pulling the cutter Mr. Macklem had restored for the short time we had it.

These were Shetlands and we were all encouraged to ride them periodically. After getting to know the ponies, riding became a delightful pastime. We would saddle them up and take them out after chores in the afternoon. Tony had been on the farm for some time and was happy to teach me how to saddle and ride. Princess was the "Spirited" one among the herd. It took me a while until I was expert enough to ride her. I was a little squeamish around her as she was the only one in the herd that ever kicked me.

She got me in the stomach, and it hurt for quite a while afterwards. There was a horseshoe shaped bruise on my stomach for weeks after that. It was my mistake. I failed to put my hand on her rump one day as I passed behind her. Princess could not be blamed for that oversight.

Princess knew the trails well though and rarely caused a ruckus while riding. On this particular day, I was pretty confident, and Tony and Donna were both riding along. I had Princess up to a good run and was well ahead of Tony and his sister. I turned around to laugh at them when I neglected to duck for a solid tree branch that crossed above the trail. Before I knew what was happening, I was on the ground, winded and little dizzy, somewhat embarrassed, but basically OK.

That wasn't much of a problem for me, but the big problem I faced at that moment was how to get Princess back. As I mentioned, she was a spirited pony and had a tendency to go her own way, which, free of me, she did. I spent the better part of my afternoon trying to chase her down to get her back to the barn.

Tony and his sister were amused by my plight and spared nothing in telling me all about it between their giggles. Finally, Mr. Macklem came out and found me in the pasture and told me to come in for dinner. He told me that Princess would find her way back to the barn when she got hungry, and I could settle her in then. He was right. Come dusk, here she comes, dragging her bridal straps behind her.

The whole time I lived there, I was only beaten once. It just wasn't in the Macklems to abuse kids. They did their best in an honest manner. But the one time I did get whooped, it was well deserved. I had asked Mr. Macklem for permission to use his tools for some project I was excited about. He allowed it with several caveats that I failed to follow and I broke a prized leather punch that I had used a hammer on.

I accidentally destroyed the punch in the process and Mr. Macklem had finally had his fill of me not doing as I was told. It was very much like my Uncle Bill's thrashing a few years before. Mr. Macklem grabbed me by my arm and led me back to the house, giving me a swift kick in the butt with each step until he finally let me go with one last kick, demanding that I go to my room. He remained there, grumbling about not being able to have nice things with Tony and I around. I had to admit that he was right. I had screwed up and he had every right to apply some discipline.

The Macklems were good people who took us to church every Sunday and didn't allow anything, at home, that Jesus Christ wouldn't approve of. Magazines, language, behavior, always treating adults with respect, all of it was enforced with a powerful look of disapproval that none of us were willing to provoke.

To this day I cannot tell you either of their first names. I'm not sure I ever knew them. It was always Mr. and Mrs. Macklem even when speaking to one another in front of us. Bathroom cleanliness was also a thing at the farm. It was always clean as a whistle, and we would hear all about it if anything was out of place when we left it.

During my stay, Mr. Macklem decided he needed a garage. Tony and I were called in to service as his construction crew. We helped with every phase of construction from pouring the cement, all the way up to tarring and Shingling the roof. One night, a storm came in and we only had three of the four walls completed and didn't have the framework for the roof on yet. We had to get out there in the wind and the rain to nail 2x4s across the top of the opening where the missing wall would soon be, to stabilize it enough that the wind wouldn't blow down the walls that we had already built.

Another project Mr. Macklem had Tony and I help him with was digging a trough for a stairwell leading to the basement of the house. We had to break out a section of the brick basement wall to install a door. It was winter and very cold and windy. The stairway was poured cement and there were times when we had to wait out there in the cold. We were way too dirty to go traipsing around in the house while we waited. It was torture, but we were all proud of what we had accomplished, once it was in and the new door had been securely attached to the basement wall. There were no leaks, either. These were skills that I would put to use several times later in life.

There were a few little cabins on the farm that were used every year to house kids from other farms during the harvest. They were vacant now but came in handy for "Camping Out" on unusually hot summer nights. They were simple wood sheds with a few bunks built into the walls. Tony and I would prop the doors open to welcome whatever cool night breeze might find its way to us.

Meals were at appointed times and if you weren't there, you missed it. We were supported in a loving manner despite what was sometimes grueling work. The Macklems believed they were building character in us, and I can't honestly testify that they had failed.

While I lived at the Macklem's, I got into the standard trouble kids get into. I was still traumatized by the implosion of my family and being unwanted. So, I imagine I was a bit more of a handful than most.

Mrs. Macklem did all the laundry, as you might imagine, and

that ended up weirding her out because of my underpants. That begs for some explanation. There is a sensation associated with needing to go to defecate. I liked the sensation and would delay going to the bathroom because of it. I didn't always correctly judge how long I could safely hold my continence, which would result in marks on my underpants. That disturbed Mrs. Macklem quite a bit and she queried me about it a few times. My reply would always be, "I don't know." because I was embarrassed about it. But also, because I didn't have the skills to articulate why it was happening.

That would happen to me many times growing up. An adult would ask me what would appear to be a simple question, the answer to which would be such a long convoluted story, that I would just act dumb out of frustration. Mrs. Macklem was genuinely disturbed by the marks on my underpants, and I suspect that it was among the reasons I was put back into the foster system.

My behavior remained effeminate and decidedly quirky in a way that I suspect made the Macklems nervous, as well. So much so, that they finally called Mr. Fox and had me put back into the system. My trauma and the ways in which it was being expressed wasn't really the Macklem's responsibility and there really wasn't a good reason why they should have taken it on. They were just trying to run a farm and do some good in the world. I hold no animus toward The Macklems for calling Mr Fox. My problems were more convoluted than they had signed up for. Not so, for Tony and Donna. They seemed seamlessly normal compared to me.

I hadn't been there for much more than a year. During that year, though, I did learn a lot of things about animals, hard work and building things, that have come in handy many a time since.

CHAPTER 10

The Schmidts

I sat on the floor in the living room losing myself in the designs in the green carpet as Mr. Fox and Mrs. Schmidt sat on the couch chatting. I wasn't listening. I had long since learned that discussions among adults about my future were none of my concern.

Mr. Fox had gathered me up from another short stay at Mrs. Rae's Children's home and brought me out here to a farm a ways outside of Memphis Michigan. As Mr. Fox and Mrs. Schmidt finished their coffee and wrapped up their conversation, I got ready to leave, hoping against hope that this was just a friendly visit between old friends. It wasn't.

Mrs. Schmidt and I walked Mr. Fox out to his Chrysler and watched as he disappeared down the highway, taking with him anything I was familiar with yesterday. I got that sinking feeling of being all alone in the world again, but this time I was able to contain it. Something just wasn't right about this, and I was uneasy about what that might turn out to be.

This was no longer a working farm but had included quite a herd of dairy cows when it was. One of the barns was equipped with stalls with water and vacuum pipes for about 40 cows. There was a grain silo attached to one end of the main barn that still had several feet of corn left in it. The place looked like the cows had all disappeared in an instant and the barn, just hosed down and left for dead. That barn would become a playground for me while I lived there.

There was only a small apple and pear orchard left that was still being maintained. A single row of a dozen pear trees ran on one side of a short road leading between the barn and the garage, past the pens, out to a grazing pasture. Apple trees lined the other.

The Schmidts were older now and rather than retire, they were in the process of buying and opening a Soda Fountain/Pool Hall in Memphis. Mrs. Schmidt was telling me about it as she gave me a short tour of the farm pointing things out as we walked. She was older and colored her already gray hair, brown. Much Like Mrs. Rae, Mrs. Schmidt wore plenty of make-up, trying in vain to mask her age. She was wiry with no shortage of energy,,, and anger, as it turned out. But today, orienting me to my new home, she seemed pleasant enough.

At the house, she showed me to the upstairs room I'd be sharing with another foster boy named Bob Logan. He was a full grown 16-year-old that was still at school when I arrived. Mrs. Schmidt asked me if I wanted to sleep in a separate bed from Bob, as there were two big beds in the upstairs room. Of course, I wanted to sleep in my own bed, but Mrs. Schmidt wasn't having it. "Well, I'm not washing two sets of sheets when it isn't necessary", she snorted. "You'll sleep here with Bob".

The next morning, Mrs. Schmidt was a whole different person. She chastised me for making such a mess in the bathroom while taking a shower last night. I doubt that I had, having learned about bathrooms at the Maclem's farm, but that didn't seem to matter. She gave me the news that I wasn't allowed to use the bathroom in the house anymore. Bob had already been living here for a while and had learned how to cope without a bathroom. It would appear that the same thing had happened to him.

We had to do our business outside, regardless of the weather and relied on leaves and corn cobs or whatever was lying around. We had to take "Bird Baths" in the utility sink by the back door. I never saw the inside of the bathroom at the Schmidt's again. It was simply off-limits.

Bob and I mainly lived in the, now vacant, chicken coop and the garage after school until the Schmidt's got back from wherever it was, they were going in the evenings. At least we got to eat at the kitchen table with them. Unless they returned late at night, which they did, sometimes. In those instances, they would usually let us sleep wherever they found us. Bob and I were rarely in the house but to eat & sleep. We were basically farm animals to the Schmidts.

It wasn't long before the beatings and sexual abuse began. Sleeping in the same bed with a horny 16-year-old was torturous for me. Bob was nearly twice my age and size, and he was violent, so there wasn't much use to resist his commands to jack him off every night. He regularly threatened to kill me if I ever told anyone what was going on. He told me that he would bury me in the back 40 and if Mr. Fox came looking for me, he would simply tell him that I ran away. I was 8 or 9 at the time and I believed his threat. I was learning how things worked at the Schmidt Farm. I was adjusting.

Bob was a troubled soul much like me, but how he coped with his trauma was very different than how I did. Bob was cruel for the sake of being cruel. When we were alone waiting for the Schmidts to come home, there was plenty of physical and sexual abuse. I guess you'd have to call it torture.

Meanwhile, Mrs. Schmidt's signature move was to grab me by my ears and lift me up and shake me. It wouldn't take much for her to do so either. She was every bit as much a sadist as Bob was. The back of my ears were always a big scab left by her fingernails that she kept opening up. I don't recall ever being beaten or physically abused by Mr.Schmidt, but unkind words and ridicule were standard operational procedure for him, and it was constant.

I walked around with bruises and little cuts and scratches from beatings most of the time I lived there. Little bruises and scratches, of course, wouldn't be out of the ordinary for farm kids. Farming is hard work and little accidents happen all the time.

The road from the Schmidt Farm to the one room school I attended went past several farms, most of which had cows in the pastures along the road. As I recall it took an awfully long time to get there from home, but in summer and fall it was beautiful. Even though I would have to walk the distance to and from school every day I looked forward to it. No one would be abusing or humiliating me for the several hours I would be at school.

It was bitterly cold in winter, and the snow would drift along the road sometimes up to my crotch and I would have to trudge through it with my big black rubber boots, with a row of buckles down the front. During the winter, there would rarely be cows in the pastures along the way, so I would sing out loud as I walked. I knew no one could hear me so I wasn't shy about it. I wasn't conscious of it at the time, but walking and singing turn out to be excellent breathing exercise.

School was, besides reading, the only joy I can recall about living with the Schmidt's. My teacher was the only person in my life at the time that treated me with any respect or dignity at all. Her name was Mrs. McGraw.

She was a tall, thin woman who I would guess was about thirty or so. She was a calm and loving soul with long but thin black hair and spoke with a slight lisp. She seemed to take a special interest in me, maybe because I didn't interact with many of the other children unless I had to. I was too busy trying to figure out some way to survive and hopefully get back to my mother someday. I got the feeling that Mrs. McGraw had some idea of what I was going through. She did, at least, have some empathy.

I was in the fourth grade at the time and was considered smart. Probably because I had nothing to do for hours after school except homework. I was called "Louis", (my middle name) at school at my own request. I wanted so badly to be someone else because my life with the Schmidts was such a carousel of depravity.

It was as if School was a parallel universe where there was no abuse, and I could actually do something right. A universe where some people liked me and treated me like I was a human being. I felt like I needed a different name for a different universe to help it feel real for those hours I spent there.

Mrs. McGraw's approval of me, over time, became paramount to my existence. She was the only one in my life who thought anything of me. She had asked me about the cuts and bruises I always had, but I was afraid to tell her. I know that she suspected something along the lines of what was happening because at School, I wasn't very accident prone and had a genteel manner. I think she might have had something to do with Mr. Fox Finding out about my being abused. I don't know that to be true, but I suspected it.

Mrs. McGraw took me aside one day and insisted that I had scrawled some obscenities on the wall inside the boy's section of the outhouse. I was innocent but she would not be convinced and told the Schmidts that not only had I done the deed but had lied to her about it as well. I couldn't understand why she was doing this to me. I was crushed by her disappointment in me. Her approval meant everything.

I was terrified about what the Schmidts would do to me when they heard about this. They were prone to beat me pretty badly for nothing, I didn't want to imagine what they would do to me if they thought I had actually done something wrong. As would be expected, I was beaten that night as well as screamed at for embarrassing the Schmidts. Strangely, the beating wasn't as fierce as I expected, but the yelling and demeaning hurt more than usual.

I cried myself to sleep that night about the injustice of it all, longing for some sort of home where I wouldn't have to deal with all the sex and mental & physical violence. That, and the back of my ears hurt from Mrs. Schmidt digging her fingernails into them.

The next day when I got to school Mrs. McGraw started in on me about how disappointed she was with me. She went on a few more times during that week about those terrible things she was sure I had written on the wall of the outhouse until it finally got to whoever had actually done it. It wasn't a student at the school, It was some former students who were now in high school.

She came to me at recess when she found out and apologized profusely for falsely accusing me and making such a fuss in front of everyone about what someone else had done. I cried for joy as she was telling me all of this because I had finally been vindicated of this crime that I had not committed and yet had suffered so much that week for. Not the least of which was the harm that had been done to the only positive relationship I had in the world at the time. The incident had changed our relationship and it was almost like a vital organ had been suddenly and forcibly ripped out of me.

Through my tears of joy and relief, I asked in earnest why she was so convinced it was me when I told her that I didn't do it. "Because, Louis, you're the only boy in this school who I know could spell those words correctly", she said.

As much as I hurt over this whole affair, I had to laugh. I assured her that I would never do anything to disappoint her like that because her approval meant so much to me. There was so little else that was positive in my life. From that day forward for the time I knew her, she considered my word, bond.

***

One average Friday when nothing out of the ordinary was happening, a man I didn't recognize came rushing into the school. He was out of breath and visibly excited. He blurted out the news that President John Fitzgerald Kennedy had been shot. The atmosphere of the whole school instantly changed to one of shocked amazement. It was as if all of us were walking around in a daze. Mrs. McGraw didn't seem to know what to do. None of us did. The man who had given us the news suggested that Mrs. McGraw send us all home to be with our families. I don't recall whether she did or not, but for the next few days, it seemed that everyone in the world was glued to their TV sets.

The Schmidt's were no exception. Our TV was tuned to CBS and they kept playing the clip of Walter Cronkite reporting that President John F. Kennedy was dead, from earlier that day. It was clear, even to me, that what was happening was not making much sense. There was something terribly wrong with what we were being told. There were convoluted and confusing reports coming at us that didn't seem to match up. The dots were not connecting.

Bob and I were in the house that whole weekend, which was rare. The beatings had stopped for those few days as our attention was otherwise occupied with the drama of the Assassination, the shooting of Oswald and the funeral procession with the rider-less horse and little John-John stepping forward to salute his father's casket rolling by.

A while after the dust had settled, Bob was entertaining a friend from school upstairs in our room. Bob and his friend were talking about school or girls or something else I wasn't the least bit interested in, so I was off in my own little world sitting at the head of our bed opposite Bob's friend. Through the half circle window above Bob's head came the only light the setting sun let in. A murky gray haze settled in the room. Bob did not turn on the light, he just continued the conversation he was having with his friend. As the conversation began to include my name I started to pay attention just a little bit.

Bob was going on about how I was his slave and that I had to do everything he said. His tone of voice got quieter as he bragged about how he made me jack him off every night and how nice it was not to have to do it himself. His friend looked at me kind of funny and told Bob he didn't believe it. He didn't even believe we slept in the same bed because he could see that there were two beds in the room.

Finally, after insisting that the story was true and realizing that his friend was just not buying it, Bob decided to demonstrate. "Get over here you little punk" he hissed. I resisted, but not because there was anything out of the ordinary about what he was going to make me do, I had jacked him off every night when we went to bed. I was very uncomfortable about the fact that he was going to make me do it while someone I didn't even know was right there in the room, watching.

Bob quickly tired of my resistance and came over to where I was, I could see from the bulge in his pants as he got up and walked towards me that he was getting hard already. He grabbed my wrist and yanked forcibly on it, snapping me to my feet. "Listen, you little fuck-up," he sneered, "when I tell you do come here, you'd better jump to it or I'll crack your jaw!" He led me roughly over to the hope chest where he had been sitting and sat down again.

His friend was quietly watching all of this. Bob sat kind of sideways on the hope chest so he could watch the stairway and talk to his friend at the same time. He unzipped his pants and put my hand on his now fully erect penis and said, "You know what to do". I continued to resist, terrified and disgusted at the prospect of doing such a thing in front of a complete stranger. It was bad enough when we were alone. Although I had learned how to almost enjoy it from having done it so many times, I still wasn't thrilled about it. My young mind just could not process having to do it while someone else watched.

I sheepishly wrapped my hand around his dick and began to stroke it like I had so many times before. I did my task while still, quietly, crying. Bob resumed talking with his friend as I worked. I wasn't paying attention to what they were saying, I was too humiliated.

Finally, Bob's friend asked him if he ever made me suck him off. My heart began to pound with fear as I heard the question because I just knew that Bob was going to make me do that too, even though we had tried it once before and my mouth wasn't big enough to contain him. Sure enough, when Bob's friend asked him that question, he went into even more of a macho control trip and said, "Sure, all the time, I'll show you". He pulled my hand away from his dick and leaned further over the railing looking to see if the coast was clear.

Then he sat back down facing his friend and pulled his knees up in front of him. He pushed his penis down between his legs and with one hand pushed me down to the floor under him. I was quietly sobbing at this point and Bob slapped me on the cheek. "Shut up you little runt" he said.

He put his hand behind my head and pushed my mouth onto his member. Fortunately, from the position he was in with his legs closed around his penis, only a short length of it was free. I was barely able to breathe, and I was beginning to panic as he pushed my head onto his dick.

I proceeded to choke on it, and I thought I might throw up for a second but as Bob loosened his grip on my head, I was at least able to breathe. Bob and his friend started laughing when I choked. Bob made me continue to suck what little of him I could contain and through the tears, disgust, and fear, I did.

Bob resumed his conversation with his friend as I worked. I went off into a trance to try and escape from the reality of what was occurring and let my mouth and body go on automatic pilot. I could vaguely hear Bob and his friend talking as I sucked. Bob's penis got harder and harder as I went along until it burst a torrent of sperm into my mouth. Bob continued talking until I backed off in terror at the flood of semen in my mouth and then burst out laughing.

When his friend realized what had happened, he joined in the laughter. I got up and quickly ran back to where I was sitting on the bed and feverishly searched for somewhere to spit out that slimy mess.

Bob, realizing what I was doing, ordered me not to spit it out and told me to swallow it. I looked at him in disbelief for a second. "Do it", he snapped. That sinking feeling of powerlessness overtook me again. I clenched my eyes closed and obsequiously swallowed. I nearly gagged. Bob and his friend laughed again and then resumed their conversation.

Simultaneously to what was happening at home and at school was a whole other drama that was happening at the pool hall. That is where I was spending most days after school.

CHAPTER 11

The Upper Room

The Schmidts picked us up at the junction of the two highways that met about a mile from the farm. That's where the school bus dropped Bob off. As we were leaving for school that morning, they had instructed us to meet them there because it was easier for them to meet us on the way into Memphis. They had purchased a pool hall/burger joint and wanted to go right to work on getting it ready to re-open. They got it for a song because the old man that owned it died in the apartment upstairs and lay there for a time before anyone discovered his body. I would guess his survivors wanted to sell it fast, probably because of just those circumstances.

When we arrived the place still reeked. We began upstairs. Mr. Schmidt and a friend of his took their sledgehammers and crow bars and dismantled the walls of the apartment while Bob and I threw all the refuse out the window to the big old truck below. I hated every moment of it because of the smell, the exertion and all the dust and plaster and nails that scratched me in a hundred places. The upside of all this is that I now had a perfectly believable explanation to tell Mrs McGraw about why I had bruises and scratches all over.

They pounded and pried and we hauled and hauled until there was one big room with bare stud walls. All that remained was the railing that encircled the stairway leading downstairs and the black canvas covered electrical wires stapled to the now bare studs. The banister post was caked with dirty black grease as if it had never been cleaned as long as the old building had stood there. A lot of the woodwork we hauled out had layers of that same grime on it. It was disgusting.

The next day, Bob and I were instructed to make a habit of meeting Mr. Schmidt after school at the junction and he would take us to the pool hall from there. For the next few days we worked on the downstairs rooms until they were cleaned, painted and somewhat remodeled.

There was one large room in the back where there were several pool tables. A dividing wall with a big opening for the billiard ball check-out counter separated the pool room from the restaurant. The front room looked just like your normal 50's soda fountain/restaurant. There was a counter with stools on one side and a row of booths on the other. Bob and The Schmidts were so excited as the place began to take shape that nobody beat or tortured me for almost a week. I was beginning to think that maybe the beatings would stop altogether. As it turned out, they were just distracted for a few days.

Finally, the time had come for the grand opening. As usual Mr. Schmidt picked us up at the junction and drove to the pool hall. Bob and Mr. Schmidt talked excitedly about the opening and how the place would be staffed, as we rode along. It was almost like they were friends. When we reached the Hall, I was ordered to go upstairs while Bob and the Schmidts opened the business to the public. I was too young to be in the pool hall when it was open because they also sold beer. Bob was too, but he could easily pass for 18.

All was well until the sun started going down. It was then that I noticed that there were no lights in the big upstairs room where I was waiting for my next instructions. There was also nowhere to sit or lay down. As a matter of fact there was no furniture of any kind in the entire room.

I sat on the floor and leaned against a stud just below a window, outside of which was a flashing neon sign. I could see the sign casting a faint red glow on the bare wood floor. From time to time, I would peek through the blinds to watch the neon light flash and try to determine if there was a pattern to the flashing. I studied how the neon tubes were bent and painted black in a few places to separate the letters from one another. It seemed so cheap and imperfect when examined that close.

I was hungry, and tired. After a while I guess I must have dozed off, because the next thing I remember was Bob yelling up the stairs to me, telling me to get downstairs so we could go home. It was dark, I couldn't see anything. They had turned off the neon sign.

As time went by, I would bring my schoolbooks home with me to have something to read. Our Teacher, Mrs. McGraw, wasn't too happy about that. I was reading way ahead of the class because I was so desperate for something to do after school. Once I told her why I was doing that, she made special arrangements with the county bookmobile to allow me to check out more than 3 books when they came around. I was allowed to check out as many as I wanted.

I remember reading Archie and Mehitabel, Stuart Little, and a couple of series I can't remember the names of about an Italian cigar smoking priest that was having engagingly comical arguments with god in the sanctuary of his church. Mrs. McGraw also suggested a mystery by Carolyn Keene called "The Secret of the Old Clock". I was suddenly in love with Nancy Drew. I would go on to read all the Nancy Drew Mysteries that the book mobile had. I would find even more of them later while I was at St Francis Home for Boys.

Reading would be a bit of a chore, in the upper room, though. I would only be able to read a few sentences while the neon light was on, I'd wait while it flashed off, and then resume reading when it flashed back on. I read like that every night for months.

I would be up there from after school until midnight when the pool hall closed.

There was electricity that fed the apartment. I could see the old braided black wires tacked to the bare 2X4s, but everything that may have been connected to them had been removed. I asked for a light and a chair or something, but nothing happened. So, I made do with the flashing neon sign.

I would imagine that someone must have told on Bob out for being underage because there were a couple times when he would be banished to the upper room with me for a night or so. Or maybe he got in trouble with the Schmidt's and that was his punishment. Either way, it was *not* a good time for me. When Bob was up there, the Schmidt's began sending us plates of food for dinner. Before that I just went without dinner some nights. It was almost like they would forget I was up there.

One night, after the Schmidts began sending plates of food up to us, Bob was upset and began taking out his frustration on me because he couldn't be downstairs with the customers. He began to masturbate and released his seed onto my dinner before making me eat it. That, evidently, didn't humiliate me enough for him, because before I was done, he stopped me and proceeded to defecate on my plate and demanded that I resume eating it, which I also did.

On our way home that night, I was unable to contain what I had been made to eat and I vomited on the floor in the back seat. The smell was obvious, and Mr. Schmidt barked back to me, "For Christ's sake, you're disgusting, Tinkerbelle. What have you been doing, eating, shit?" The comment elicited a momentary gale of laughter from Bob and Mrs. Schmidt followed by complaints about the smell. I remained silent, remembering Bob's threat about telling on him.

Moments later, we were home. Everyone quickly got out of the car and Mrs. Schmidt grabbed me by my ears, digging her fingernails into the backs of them. She lifted me off the ground, still holding me by my ears, and shook me vigorously. She was demeaning me for soiling the car. Not that she needed much of a reason to demean me. It was her resting pulse. She ordered me to stay out there and clean the car while she and the others went to bed.

Shortly thereafter at the pool hall, the Schmidts put a light bulb in a bare socket attached to what I can only guess was a swag lamp at one point. But today it was just a socket on a zip cord dangling from the ceiling on a cup hook. And, it worked, which drew a heavy sigh of relief from me and that stack of books that were taking me way too long to read. Those books were my only respite from the rest of my tortured life and starting today that was going to be a little easier to do. I must admit, I was quietly excited about it.

The excitement would be short lived, however, because Bob, bored again, ceremoniously pulled down the light from its hook and dramatically unscrewed the bulb watching for my reaction. He was telegraphing that he intended to do something to me with it. He walked over to me and ordered me to put my dick in the live socket. I tried to resist for a minute, but I knew that I would have to do it, I was trapped! Where I was and the environment I lived in was a "Do or Die" world that he alone was in control of. I still had a will to live, and I was determined to do so. He handed me the socket and ordered me again to stick my dick in it.

With adrenaline rushing and a sense if mortal dread, I finally did.

I don't know how long I was out, but when I came to, Bob seemed nervous and apprehensive. I don't think he said another word that evening. I was feeling oddly relieved. I was calm but felt drained like you do after a particularly vigorous workout. I got up, screwed the light bulb back into the socket and proceeded to string it back up. It was going to come in handy when the sun was completely down.

The worst night, though, was while Bob was still, or again, banished to the upper room, he was mad at me about something. Who knows what that might have been? He wouldn't need much of a reason to be mad at me. It probably wasn't even me he was mad at.

What I do recall was Bob lifting me up by my ears like he had seen Mrs. Schmidt do so many times. Only this time, he was leaning against the banister and dangling my squirming body over the open stairwell. I was terrified by his anger and my precarious predicament as he threatened to drop me. I had this sinking gut-wrenching feeling that this is going to be it for me. He was going to kill me. My entire existence was an uproarious jumble of hysterical deadly terror. I believed I was facing my death. To his credit, he didn't drop me down the stairs. I dodged that bullet; for now, anyway.

There were plenty more incidents like these that populated my life with the Schmidts. I could pretty much expect to be abused in some way, by one or more of these three people on almost a daily basis. Sometimes the violence would stop for a few days. I knew what that meant! That meant that Mr. Fox would be stopping by sometime soon to check on me.

While living with the Schmidts I don't recall ever hearing a kind word from any of them. It was always ridicule, sex and violence. They seemed to derive some twisted satisfaction from beating and humiliating me.

Christmas with the Schmidts was no exception. This time, it was humiliation. Like in any normal family, everyone was excited for weeks leading up to Christmas. I didn't expect much of the holiday, but I did want to participate. Christmases back home were warm and exciting. We had rules where we would be able to open one gift on Christmas Eve but couldn't open any more until the whole family was present on Christmas Day. We would hear one of the parents read "The Night Before Christmas" to us before turning in and trying to sleep. There would be Christmas Carols and ginger snaps and hot cocoa with marshmallows. The next day, there would be stockings full of candy and little toys and lots and lots of gifts to open when all the family had finally arrived. But that was long ago.

It wasn't like that at the Schmidt's. Bob had threatened to kill me if I got a gift for anyone. He even told people that I didn't intend to get anything for anyone because I was so selfish. He was setting me up for the torture he intended to inflict on me for Christmas. There were no stockings, no poems, no Christmas Carols, no big dinner where us kids had to sit at a smaller, lower table set up just for us.

When Christmas Day arrived, we were all sitting in the Living room while everyone was exchanging gifts, except me. There were The Schmidts, their 2 grown sons and their kids and wives gathered in the living room around the sparsely decorated tree. Each time someone would open a gift, Bob would make some sort of remark pointing out that none of the gifts were from me. This would occasionally evoke similar comments from some of the others who were gathered.

Bob had gotten me a Michigan State Sweatshirt that was the only present I received. He laid it on thick as he handed it to me. "Here," he said, with a sneer, "even though you're so selfish, I got you something anyway!"

The comments hurt like stab wounds as I sat there on the floor stewing in my degradation. Not only was I forbidden to give a gift to anyone, but I couldn't even explain why. I just had to sit there wallowing in humiliation. I get a little weird around Christmas time, partly because of what that specific Christmas was like for me. It brings up some truly ugly feelings for me. It wouldn't be the only sad and uncomfortable Christmas for me, but it was probably the worst.

It wasn't until later that evening that I learned that the sweatshirt Bob had given me was much too big for me. That's because it was never actually for me. Once we were upstairs in our room, Bob unceremoniously repossessed it.

CHAPTER 12

The Day From Hell

The Schmidts had 2 grown sons, or maybe they were previously foster kids. One, Eric, was a family man with 2 boys and the other was a bachelor who lived in a mobile home and drove a Corvette. I don't remember his name. I had never met him before this day that we were at his trailer to gather him up for some event later that day.

In hindsight, he was a perfect trailer park redneck womanizer type, though much better looking than one might imagine. He dressed well and clearly took care of himself. I got the impression that he was a somewhat troubled soul from how the Schmidts treated him. It was with the same kind of disdain with which they treated me and Bob. I think they were so critical of him because he was an alcoholic or something. He seemed defiant to their complaints.

The other son, Eric, was clearly an upwardly mobile type; a married first-time home buyer, enjoying the fruits of the auto manufacturing boom that Detroit and Flint were famous for. The home was new. You could see that the grass hadn't even come in yet. The lawn was cordoned off with string to indicate where grass would eventually be. The house was almost rural, as there were precious few houses around us. It was a housing development in progress. One could see where the houses would someday stand, but at this moment in time, they had not yet been built. We were out there pretty much alone.

There was some sort of all-day adults only event that the folks were going to. That left me, Bob Logan and the 2 boys alone at Eric and his family's new home. Bob was to babysit the rest of us because he was the oldest.

Over the course of the day, Bob taught the boys how to tie me up, naked, into uncomfortable positions and take turns beating and kicking me. I think the boys were told to urinate on me at one point and I recall being stuffed into a refrigerator in the basement for a while and then hung from a rafter by my feet, all while still being tied up and naked. Throughout the day, that seemed to go on forever, I fluctuated between abject terror and resignation that I would never make it through this day. I would get real calm, periodically during the day, with the realization that I would be dead soon and the horror would come to an end.

At some point late in the day, the side of my head got injured and began to bleed. That stopped the torture for a while so Bob and the boys could work on stopping the bleeding. Shortly after they got the bleeding stopped, the parents arrived. They were all drunk. From the condition of the house, it was clear that we had been up to no good and they were *not* pleased.

Mrs. Schmidt took charge and lined all of us up in the kitchen for some discipline, Schmidt style. She was uncharacteristically sharp with Bob and may have even slapped him. He wasn't talking about what happened.

When she got to me, still holding a drink that she absolutely did not need, she demanded that I tell her what had been happening all day. In response to my silence, she threw the drink in my face and asked me again. I still remained silent, recalling Bob's mortal threat. This is a life and death world I live in. Besides that, I knew there would be no comfort there, for the life changing experience I had just been through.

I was exhausted, but there was a gently simmering feeling of relief borne of the fact that I was still alive. I was sure that if I talked, Mrs. Schmidt would have found a way to make it out to be my fault.

Finally realizing that I wasn't going to tell her, she slapped me hard. The slap banged my head against a jutting corner of the kitchen wall, re-opening the injury Bob and the boys had just gotten to stop bleeding. It started bleeding again, this time a little worse than before. This seemed to anger Mrs. Schmidt even more and as the other adults tended to my injury; she was angrily demanding that I clean up the mess my bleeding was making on the new kitchen floor. Eric and his wife, tending to my injured head, glared at her incredulously.

***

It was one of Mr. Fox's responsibilities to come around from time to time to check up on his charges to see how they were getting along in their foster placements. I assumed that he would call ahead to let the Schmidts know when he was coming, because the beatings would stop for a few days before he arrived. I never really made the connection until that fateful day when he apparently *didn't* call ahead.

Mr. Fox must have suspected that something was up the last few times he had come by because I would have seemed more distant and closed than he was used to. There were always little bruises and scratches that remained from my mistreatment, but I was a little kid living on a farm. That kind of thing would normally be expected. He was a little suspicious and would always ask about them, but I wouldn't tell him anything for fear of being killed. I would just make up something that sounded believable to explain my injuries. He would nervously get into his white Chrysler, that I liked so much, and return to Port Huron.

It was shortly after my day in hell that Mr. Fox showed up at the Schmidt's Farm unannounced. It had been a particularly bad week for beatings and abuse and my injuries from that horrible day at Eric's house were still fresh enough to be plainly visible. I was coming home from school and Mr. Fox was already there, in the driveway, sitting in his car. He got out and approached me as I walked up the driveway.

He examined the back of my ears and the gash in the side of my head. There were other minor scratches and bruises like I always had from the beatings and abuse I had somehow survived. But Mr. Fox went directly to the injuries I sustained at Eric's house.

He ordered me into the front seat of his car and drove away without a word to the Schmidts. I often wonder if Mrs. McGraw had figured out how to contact him. By this time, she was reasonably sure there was something untoward going on at the Schmidt farm. I wondered if he had already spoken with the Schmidts before I arrived, because as soon as he saw me coming, he knew exactly where to look on my body to assure himself that there was indeed a problem.

As we rode back to Mrs. Rae's Children's Home, I finally broke down and tearfully told Mr. Fox everything that had happened, including the sex and abuse and why I didn't tell him what was going on. Mr. Fox was angrily grinding his teeth and looking straight ahead as he drove, listening to my horrific tale. He assured me over and over that I would never have to see the Schmidts again. I am absolutely certain that Mr.Virgil Fox saved my life that day. I have no doubt that had I remained with the Schmidts, they would have eventually killed me.

CHAPTER 13

St Francis Infirmary

As we rode along in Mr. Fox's white Chrysler that I liked so much, he was telling me about his good friend, Sister Delores. Evidently, she was the Reverend Mother of St Francis Home for Boys in Detroit Michigan. In fact, that's where Mr. Fox was taking me at that very moment. He was chattering on about how much I was going to like St Francis and how much fun I could look forward to having with all the other boys there. Although I found his voice soothing, I wasn't really listening. My agenda was a little different than Mr. Fox's.

The last pair of shoes that had been handed down to me at Mrs. Rae's Children's Home evidently had some sort of fungus or something that turned the ends of my toes into gooey looking weeping sores that stuck to my socks. They hurt awfully badly but that wasn't even the main thing on my mind as Mr. Fox prattled on about St Francis Home for Boys. What was foremost in my mind was how much this was looking like yet another stop on what was beginning to look like an endless journey taking me further and further away from the one thing, in all the world, that I so deeply longed for. I wanted to go home. I didn't realize at the time that home, as I knew it, didn't even exist anymore.

Try as I might, I couldn't make anyone in charge understand that I wasn't interested in fun, new friends, school, cameras, radios, ice cream, carnival rides, baseball cards, zoo animals, movies, or looking to the future. I was focused on getting my swishy little ass back home. I wanted my mom back!

Unfortunately, that was the one thing Mr. Fox and the state of Michigan, with all of its resources, could not materialize. All of this talk about Sister Delores and all the fun I was going to have was falling on deaf ears and I'm pretty sure Mr. Fox knew it.

As we approached St. Francis, I was stricken by the sheer size of it. It was a grand looking brick building with sweeping arches and a row of what looked like turrets along the top; like you might see along the top of old European castles. What I learned later was that these "Turrets" were the alcove windows of the dorm I would be living in. It resembled something right out of a medieval adventure movie. I half-expected somebody like Errol Flynn or Peter O'Toole to come swashbuckling out from behind the building on a big white horse to save the day. The fact that it was a somewhat cloudy and misty day, probably contributed to the imaginings I was having in my head. I was suddenly a visiting dignitary on a secret mission for Queen Elizabeth and I was being escorted by the trusty knight, Sir Virgil of Foxworth, who had been dispatched to provide for my protection on the journey.

Just as my mind got started filling in the rest of the story, the car came to a stop in front of the steps leading to the big oak doors of the entrance. Mr. Fox turned off the car and turned to me to reassure me one last time that I was going to love it here. This time I think he was saying it more for himself than for me. I'm reasonably sure that by now, he knew that trying to get me excited about moving to yet another strange place was a lost cause.

The meeting with Sister Delores was a short one. All the arrangements about my move had already been made. Sister Delores began to echo what Mr. Fox had been telling me on the way over. I was going to have the most wonderful time here! Mr. Fox told her about the sores on my feet.

They excused themselves and stepped out of the room for a moment for some confidential discussion, leaving me with another nun, who was probably there as a receptionist. I was not the least bit concerned about their departure or their secrecy. I had long since become accustomed to it. You might say that it was standard operational procedure by that time. Decisions would be made by adults charged with my care about where I would live and go to school and whom would be responsible for me. None of that would be within my purview. I was being moved around from place to place for reasons that would be invisible to me.

Meanwhile, in the reception area, the Nun was making some announcements on the intercom and noticed that I seemed interested, which I was, and she began to explain how the intercom worked. She had barely begun when the two returned. Mr. Fox assured me one last time, that I would be fine.

He said his goodbyes and left by the door we had just come in. As the door closed behind him, my heart sank with the realization that I was, once again, all alone in a strange place. It was as if my escape route back to anything familiar was sealed shut with the sound of that big oak door closing behind him.

I started crying. Sister Delores tried to comfort me, and she was a professional. That's what nuns do, for heaven's sake, but my eyes simply would not obey me and proceeded to flood with tears despite my best efforts.

I so very deeply hated this feeling of being alone in a place where there was absolutely nothing that remained of yesterday, except this longing that I was now so familiar with. I had prayed over and over that all this shuffling around would one day end, but it never did. Once again there was that feeling that, this time, could not be held back until I could be alone to cry it out privately.

Sister Delores led me, still crying, down a few hallways and through a choir loft in a chapel, to the infirmary. She gently held her hand on my shoulder the entire way from the lobby and spoke quietly as we walked.

She told me that the sisters there would look after my feet and see if they could make them better. Little did I know that as she turned me over to the nuns in the infirmary that I would not see her again, face to face, until over a year later when I would be embroiled in a censorship scuffle over an article I had written for a school newspaper I had founded.

That first night, I laid there in yet another unfamiliar bed. The nuns had bathed me, fed me and encouraged me into a clean pair of someone's old pajamas. I guess I should have been grateful, and maybe somewhere inside, I was. But the unfamiliarity with my surroundings and the fact that there was absolutely no one in this new world that I knew yesterday, made me feel so empty.

After putting me to bed, the sisters turned off the lights and went somewhere I couldn't see, the infirmary became very quiet. For a while, I watched a moth flutter silently around an exit light just across the hall from the room I was in. The little guy kept bumping into the glass trying in vain to get closer to the source of the light. I knew the feeling.

The dim reddish light from the exit sign reflecting off the prison gray paint on the ceiling created a brooding brown wash that shown down on my face just bright enough to keep me awake for a while. All was quiet but for the sound of water running through some old pipes nearby. I could vaguely hear voices from another room just barely loud enough to be audible but not loud enough to make out any words. The voices seemed jovial, and it made me wish I felt differently.

As I had often done on my first night in a new place, I began to review my life up to that point. I desperately tried to figure out what I had done, or what I had lacked that kept me away from the people I loved. I hated the fact that I was effeminate and obsequious and there didn't seem to be anything I could do about it. I was doing the best I could, and it felt like I was never enough to belong anywhere. What could I have done that was so bad? Why doesn't my mom come and get me and take me home? Where are my brother Mike and my cousins? What will become of me?

The questions piled up, unanswered, like so many dishes on the counter by the sink. I could no longer contain the longing. My tears, as if by their own volition, quietly flowed down my face to the pillow. I tried, like I always do, to keep it quiet so as not to attract any attention to my deep loneliness. It was too uncomfortable to try to explain to total strangers what I had been through up to now; what it felt like to be unwanted by my parents and separated from my brother and my cousins. I wondered what they were thinking about me being gone like this.

Lying there, I was recalling how many times I had found myself in this same situation over and over. I wondered if it would ever end. I was crying for someone familiar to hold me and tell me everything would be alright. But, of course, no one came. Everything would not always be alright.

One of the nuns must have heard me sniffling and came to the door of the room. "Are you crying?" she whispered. "No", I quietly lied. She gave me that look. You know the one. That compassionate motherly look that I think they must teach in nun's school. They can all do it. I tried to deny that anything was wrong, but the woman was undeterred. She sat in the chair near the end of the bed and rested a calming hand on my ankle. She began to talk. She had a kind demeanor and her voice was soothing, so I let her go on even though I'd have preferred to cry alone.

She was telling me she knew how I felt, left all alone in the world with no one to turn to. "But", she said, "There are parents who will never desert you, who will be there for you whenever you need them and they will never, ever leave you." She told me a few stories about Mary, the mother of Jesus, and God the Father.

Of course, I knew about them already, but I had never put them into quite that context before. As she continued to tell me about how loving and nurturing, I could expect Mother Mary to be and how much Mary wanted me to be her son, just like Jesus was, it began to make sense to me.

My crying slowed down as I gradually began listening more intently to what she was saying. "Could this be possible?" I thought. Or is this just another ploy to get me to accept what was happening to me even though I knew it wasn't right for someone to have to go through this over and over. As I lay there listening to her go on about Mary and Jesus and God the Father I began to relax, and eventually fell asleep.

When I woke the next morning, there on the chair where the nun had been sitting last night, was a little plastic, glow in the dark, statue of Mother Mary and a little book of prayers. As I wiped the sleep from my eyes a little bit of calm came over me.

Although I wasn't really into this, something inside of me felt like this wouldn't be so bad after all. Maybe I *could* pick myself up and try to find some good in all of this. Maybe even enjoy myself a little. I was here and I was still alive. Given what I had been through, I knew very well that my life *could* be even worse.

That little statue remained a constant companion through my time at St Francis. It was just barely small enough to fit in my pocket. I remember how it used to delight me that I could hold her up to the light before going to bed and then get under the covers when they turned out the dorm lights. I could see her features, so kind and gentle, glowing so clearly. Sometimes just having that statue made me feel a little bit better. I do not recall if I ever saw the nun who gave it to me, again.

CHAPTER 14

St Francis Academy

As both Mr. Fox and Sister Delores had foreseen, there were times when I had to admit that I was enjoying myself. I made a few close friends, and we created our own little society apart from the others who teased us and called us names all the time. It was good to have friends. It blunted the sting of the cajoling that was central to my social life in group living.

Mrs. Judith Herzog was assigned as my case worker at St Francis. She was a young and slightly chubby woman with a pleasant manner about her. She had beautiful green eyes and a heart like a bottomless pit in its capacity to care. She always, and I do mean *always*, wore her light brown hair in a tight French twist, with a little sprig of bangs that she carefully swept to one side in a tidy little swoosh like the Nike logo. Her demeanor, when around me, was casual and relaxed in a way that seemed in stark contrast to the rigid and meticulous care she obviously put into her appearance.

Mrs. Herzog was always on the look-out for something to get me involved with to redirect my attention from how tortured I was about not being wanted by my family. She was another in a steady flow of people in my life that were trying to give me anything and everything except the one thing I so deeply longed for!

She knew I had a little transistor radio that I seemed to guard jealously. It was always tuned to WKNR Keener 13. They played a lot of Motown, which I loved. I would put it under my pillow at night and listen quietly until I fell asleep.

***

At St Francis, each of us was required to carry a "Demerit Card". It was about the size of a business card. We had to carry it at all times and we were required to produce it on demand. A superior would make a mark in one of the tiny boxes on the card if we had misbehaved in some way. We were given a new one each week.

Mrs. Herzog told me about a record player she had that she never used and asked if I might like to have it. I was interested in a big way. She told me that I would have to show her three consecutive demerit cards with no more than one mark. Once I did that, she would give it to me. It took me a while, but I did it and she did give me the record player.

It was a really nice one too, a very early portable stereo record player. It weighed a ton and was nestled its own cabinet that looked like a suitcase and was about as big. The 2nd speaker clipped on to one end of it. While at St Francis, though, it had to be kept in the property cage and I could only get to it with permission from Sister Lucille and only on my free time. It was one of only a few items I took with me when I graduated.

One of my few friends at St Francis was named Frank Matsco. A heavy-set boy that was too big for his age. He had wavy black hair and dark brown eyes like mine. He was, in every sense of the word, a boy, an easily excitable boy. I'm pretty sure he was developmentally delayed, though I didn't have a word for it at that age. We hit it off right away. I sensed a kinship with him because he clearly wasn't into being a tough guy like his size might indicate. He was the gentle giant in our little clique; our own "Baby Hughie".

The other boys gave him the nickname "Heatwave" alluding to the pop song by Martha Reeves & The Vandellas. The first time I saw him get angry; the reason for the nickname became vividly clear. When the other boys' teasing or harassment would build up to the point where it became too much for him, he would fly into a fit of frustrated rage and begin spinning around flailing his arms about and making a sound that was kind of like squealing and grunting simultaneously.

It would take the nuns a while to calm him down. To me, it was a cruel, pitiful, and frightening thing for a kid like me to have to watch and it happened quite a bit. But many of the other boys found it funny and would provoke him just to get him to do it. Matsco was a decent sort, though, and one of my few real friends.

Another boy in our little group was named "Tobias". In group settings we were always referred to by our last names because first names were all too common. I'm sure Tobias had a first name, but I don't think I ever knew it, or cared to. He was nearly Matsco's opposite. Tobias had fiery flashing blue eyes and too many teeth for a mouth that size. He had curly brown hair and slight build. Aside from not wearing glasses, he looked like the textbook image of a nerdy little Jewish boy. I liked Tobias a lot. He was such a buoyant spirit and was always kind to me.

He could be counted on to include me in any wild scheme he would come up with, and there were many. But he would rarely pursue it if I thought it was a dumb idea. Matsco, being my right-hand man, would never be talked into anything I didn't think was cool either. So I guess I was kind of the gatekeeper for our group.

One idea that Tobias got me into was pretending to be a famous rock band from England like The Beatles or the Rolling Stones. They were all the rage at that time. We brainstormed for a while on that one.

We decided to make these musical instruments out of cardboard boxes and whatever else we could get our hands on. We got so caught up in this that even Sister Lucille, who held us in as much disdain as everyone else, found herself helping us out by letting us cut up one of the old barrels used for sweeping compound and got us some old mop heads from the janitor that we cut up to look like those British rock stars.

We cut the barrel up in sections and covered both ends with paper which gave us a passable fake drum set. Tobias had an old broomstick that he taped a cardboard drawing of a guitar to. He even pasted some strings on it using some yarn. I had the simple task of cutting a cardboard box to look like an organ. It took 2 cuts in a straight line over one edge of the box and I just pushed it in and drew keys on it. Done! It looked vaguely like one of those Farfisha Organs that were so popular at the time.

Finally, when all was ready, we talked Sister Lucille into arranging to have my record player for a few hours. We went all around the division telling everyone who would listen that we were going to have a show in the crafts room. We put a record on and proceeded to lip-sync to it, pretending to play these instruments we had just made.

Roughly 15 to 20 boys showed up to watch this spectacle. About halfway through the first song, I began to feel thoroughly stupid, like I had let myself get suckered into making myself look like even more of a total idiot in front of a whole room full of kids who already thought I was well on my way there to begin with.

I wanted to cry and run away as fast and as far as I could. Tobias must have sensed that I was coming apart at the seams and tried his best to get me to enjoy the whole scene by looking me hard right in the eye and getting even more into the illusion. "Please don't fall apart now", he seemed to be pleading. His unspoken encouragement must have been all I needed because, somehow, I continued and I'm still here to tell you about it. It's a LOT more fun remembering it now, than it was to be there doing it, though. The other kids appeared to like this whole fantasy. There was a smattering of applause. However, I'm sure it was a lot more for The Beatles' songs than for our corny little imitation of them.

***

Another time, I had evidently written a cool essay at school or something because when Mrs. Herzog found out about it, she questioned me about my interest in writing. We kicked the topic around for a few minutes and I decided to start a school newspaper. Mrs. Herzog corralled the office staff to help with the project.

Me Tobias and Matsco were the entire staff of "The St Francis Telstar". I had hand drawn a masthead that went down the side of the front page and listed all three of us as the staff of the paper. The nuns in the administrative office taught me how to use a mimeograph machine and provided paper and secretarial help.

In the third and last edition, I had written a story about a student that had an epileptic seizure while sliding down a banister on the stairway. He ended up falling off the banister and was flopping around on the floor like a fish out of water. I could tell it was serious and it struck me deeply. I immediately went rushing to write it all down. Sister Delores, apparently tipped off by one of the nuns helping us, read it before we took it out to distribute it, and objected to the story.

She told us we couldn't distribute it as it would be an embarrassment to the boy who had the seizure; maybe even traumatize him. I cried censorship and Mother Delores and I argued back and forth for what seemed like a long time.

Finally, Mother Delores threw up her hands and brought the hammer down on my lead story. It was a no-go. I gave up the idea of the newspaper when I realized that I was not going to be permitted to report the news. Besides that, Mr. Longo wasn't very happy about our little newspaper, mainly because he didn't like any of the three of us that had created it. I'll go into that a little later. But it was an engaging ride while it lasted, and Mother Delores now knew who I was.

***

Though he wasn't one of our little group, Clifford Reynolds was a figure in Division 4. This tall thin gracefully quiet and unassuming older boy was a year ahead of us. His height, his coal black skin and eyes, made him stand out among the multiracial swarm of schoolboys residing at St. Francis. He was our platoon leader. He always carried himself with a kind of humility, like he was trying, in vain, not to be noticed. He was a model of good behavior, too. His demerit card was much cleaner than mine, or anyone else's, for that matter.

There were about 40 of us in my section, all 7th and 8th graders. I was quite some distance from being one of the cool kids. You know the ones; the football players, the smart kids, the class clowns, the more confident, less damaged boys among us. The boys who excelled at something. Although he was certainly one of them, he wasn't really connected to any of us. He seemed so solitary. I can't think of anyone that he would hang out with on a regular basis, almost like he didn't have a best friend. He seemed more like an adornment on the whole platoon, a decoration, if you will. He seemed more like one of the adults.

The only time I ever saw him loose his cool was one of those nights when Sister Mary Frances was away and we were all alone in our dorm room on the top floor. As one would expect, when the cat's away, the mice will play. That would happen from time to time while I lived there.

Ordinarily, the absence of an adult would strike fear into my very soul. That would mean that the Alpha boys among us would be free to terrorize people like me and my few friends. But this time, Reynolds was there and everyone kind of idolized him. We could relax a little bit because we knew Reynolds looked down on such bullying behavior.

After showers, Michael Brady was dancing on his bunk wearing a towel wrapped high around his slight frame covering his little chest, down to his knees, like it was a sexy evening gown. He had pulled a pair of white socks over his hands and forearms like evening gloves. He climbed up on his bed and began mimicking a singer on stage. Most of us thought this hysterically funny and our laughter was both quick and animated.

Except Clifford Reynolds. As Reynolds walked into the dorm from his shower and witnessed this impromptu drag show, he instantly began chasing Brady around the dorm screaming at him in a menacing manner. Brady, who was now in fear for his life, took off like a cartoon character scrambling around lockers and under bunks trying to avoid what we all thought would surely be his demise. The laughter immediately stopped, as no one had ever seen Reynolds lose it like this and he was nearly twice Brady's height.

Fortunately, for young Michael Brady, he was smaller and much quicker than the towering Reynolds. I suppose there's a psychological breakdown about why Reynolds reacted to this joke so vociferously. It was so unlike him. I mean Brady was a kid just trying to have a little fun. Reynolds, finally, came back to himself and gave up the chase, but made no secret of his displeasure and loudly ordered Brady to remove the offending costume and to do so with a quickness. Which, or course, Brady did, sheepishly cowering by his locker, fearing another outburst of Clifford's rage, that never came. My guess was that Reynolds must have had some experience with drag queens that traumatized him and it just never came up before. It was a surprise to everyone; maybe even to Reynolds himself.

Being one of the cool kids in a military school, Reynolds was a football player and was also in ROTC. A good student and a natural leader, he was noticed by more than the other boys in our platoon. Teachers and prefects also showered a lot of attention on the young star.

His graduation, a year ahead of mine, was a time of stress and anxiety for all of us. He was our golden boy and had injured his ankle in the playground a few days before graduation. Our graduation included field day demonstrations of formation marching, rifle drills and other displays of military decorum. He was in a lot of pain and, because he was our platoon leader, we were all depending on him to lead us through our paces.

At the time, it felt like the whole Academy was on pins and needles wondering if he would be able to stand on his own two feet for the ceremony. Reynolds, too, was worried. For those few days, the rest of us, staff and student alike, worked together in doing whatever we could to pamper him and clear away any distractions to his recovery.

When the day came, Reynolds was still in pain. Sister Lucille wanted to bench him for the ceremony because he was still a bit shaky on his feet. He insisted that he would be fine, and proceeded, through his pain, to perform with his usual grace and decorum. That's the kind of guy he was.

Among orphans like us, it was like we were sending our best champion forward onto the world as proof of our worth as little men, which was clearly not what the world's lowered expectations of us would suggest we were capable of. He was our golden child and he demonstrated why during that graduation ceremony.

Meanwhile, I was definitely *not* a golden child. I woke up one morning with a turd wrapped up in a handkerchief beside me in bed. I had to miss breakfast because I had to stay behind to take a shower, put on fresh clothes and bundle my bedding and pajamas up and take it all down to the laundry.

By that time, Breakfast was over, and it was time to go to school. That little prank happened quite a few times. Thankfully, it only happened to me once. Whoever was doing it was evidently into "spreading the love" and doing it to other boys too.

The other prank pulled on me more than once was being short sheeted. To Short sheet someone is to arrange the top sheet on a bed in a way that leaves no space for the feet of a person attempting to get into it. After the first few times it happened to me, I took to carefully inspecting my bed before attempting to get in it.

At St. Francis, I was subjected to the same kind of mental and physical bullying I had experienced in other group settings which extended my trauma. But for others, these were just juvenile pranks. Those of us that were the butt of others' chiding lived in terror on those nights when Sister Mary Francis was away. The alpha boys among us were effectively released to abuse the rest of us at will. St. Francis offered no more protection from occasional nights of terror, than any other group placement I had found myself in.

There were, what I guess one would call "Stoners", at St. Francis as well. They were the kids that would get a hold of enough alcohol to get drunk or put model airplane glue or spray paint in a paper bag and breathe the fumes. I recall Eddie Wenzell, on another of those nights when the cat was away, stumbling down the aisle between the 2 rows of bunks in a feigned panic, shouting that he was shrinking. He had likely put on someone else's pajamas that were clearly too big for him. He woke us all up with his stoned and comedic demonstration. But if we had to be woken up in the middle of the night, at least we got some entertainment out of it. It was quite funny to watch.

After Reynolds graduated from St Francis, a new seargent needed to be chosen. McDonald had been chosen to lead us. Evidently Sister Lucille saw some leadership qualities in him that she thought that he might be able to keep us all in line. He was a black kid in my grade. He wasn't particularly bigger or smaller than most of us and he was definitely one of the alpha boys and tough as nails. People didn't mess with him because he had an aura about him that signaled not to do so.

It wasn't long before his leadership style began to emerge. His style of leadership was based on instilling fear and intimidation. Sister Lucille let this go on for a few weeks, I would guess, to let McDonald, or the rest of us, work it out on our own. After a few weeks of this, the whole division was on edge about how we were being bullied by this guy. This was a military environment and we had all been trained that you have to follow orders of a superior officer and there's no two ways about it. When it became clear to her that the situation was not working itself out, Sister Lucille had to step in.

She called the entire division into the play room for a "Come to Jesus" moment. I don't think she knew who to replace McDonald with, but she knew that his reign of terror had to end and it was going to end tonight. She ceremoniously cleared out a big circle in our midst and threw down 2 pairs of boxing gloves in the middle of it. She stepped back and dressed down McDonald for being such a bully and them challenged anyone in the group to stand up to him.

McDonald leaned confidently against a locker with his arms crossed against his chest and just glared at all of us. It was like he was saying, "You think you can take me? Bring it on!" You could hear a pin drop as the silence got longer and longer. Nobody was moving and you could cut the tension with a knife.

***

Jefferson was a little red-headed boy a grade behind me. Besides Tobias, he was probably the smallest kid in the division. He had been nicknamed "Mouse" for good reason. He was usually quiet, unassuming and well behaved. It was almost like he wanted to get through school without being noticed. He was somehow able to sidestep being bullied by the alpha boys despite his diminutive size. Everything about him was a projection of a desire for righteous peace.

***

The silence became deafening as it continued. Finally, Jefferson sheepishly crept into the center of the circle, like he was trying not to be noticed, and slowly put a pair of the gloves on. He just stood there in the middle of the circle with his gloved hands dangling loosely at his sides in resignation. Finally, he quietly spoke. "This is wrong!", he said through his welling up tears. "Somebody has to do something about this and if none of you will, then I guess it will have to be me. But it *has* to stop tonight." Sister Lucille nodded approvingly as Jefferson pulled himself up straighter with a look of fear, courage and determination in his eyes. It was clear to everyone that McDonald could lay this little guy out with one punch. Even Jefferson knew it.

McDonald immediately let his arms fall to his sides and rolled his eyes as he looked up a little in resignation. It was like he was admitting defeat. He didn't say anything, but it was clear that he was not going to fight Jefferson. Maybe it was Jefferson's courage, his determination or his willingness to march into hell to make the terror stop for all of us. Or, maybe it was just the man that Jefferson had become in that moment. McDonald looked at Sister Lucille obviously wondering what to do. Sister Lucille returned his look and quietly asked, "Well?" There was a pause and then McDonald said "I'm not going to fight him!"

The room immediately erupted into applause and cheering. Most of the room gathered around Jefferson and raised one of his arms in victory. Mouse had slayed the dragon! After a few minutes, Sister Lucille quieted the room down and said, "Jefferson, you're a Sargent now. Get your division in formation and get them upstairs to bed." The poor fellow hadn't a clue of what to do, but he had the support of the whole division. We did know what to do and we did it with sharp precision. We quickly fell in and waited at attention for his command.

McDonald changed that night. After the confrontation, he seemed more relaxed and didn't threaten people like he had previously. He was humble in a way that we hadn't seen in him before. He even made friends with me and some of my group. It was like night had changed to day. I think he may have learned something about himself that night and maybe it meant something to him.

As you've probably guessed, Sargent Jefferson quickly got himself up to speed and learned how to shout orders loud enough for all of us to hear. His leadership style was to be a good example and it worked well. There was peace in the division with scant few exceptions for that whole last year of my residence there. He lived up to his reputation as a hero to his peers.

CHAPTER 15

Mr. Longo & ROTC

Mr. Longo was our 7th & 8th grade teacher and took on extra duties in relation to us cadets that would require an adult male. That included Physical Ed, shower supervision, field trips and the like. Though I doubt that Mr. Longo had ever served in the military, he was also our ROTC trainer. A Pedophile, he looked like he might have been middle eastern with his close cropped black hair, deep dark eyes, olive skin and hawk-like facial features.

He held me in a kind of contempt and made no secret of his disfavor. Like the time I had created a school newspaper, "The St. Francis Telstar", and proudly brought a stack of them to class for distribution. Rather than distribute them, Mr. Longo set the stack on a windowsill by an open window. After briefly making fun of me and the paper, he reached over and pushed the stack out the window with a dramatic flourish. The breeze spread them all over the front lawn of the academy. "There, Honey, now they are distributed." he sneered.

It was clear that this display was at least partly theater designed for the rest of the class to enjoy. And, they did! To me, it was just standard operational bullying, and it hurt. When Mr. Longo was in charge, it was often like when the nuns would occasionally be away and we were left on our own. He would turn loose the dogs of war on us as if we were altogether unsupervised.

Mr. Longo had only approached me for sex on one occasion.

It was during school one day. He had heard from one of my classmates that I had jacked off Alan Soriano the night before. It was one of those times when Sister Mary Frances was away, and we were all on our own. Soriano was a Polynesian lad who was among the very elite of cool cadets. He was beautiful to me and had a graceful, shapely body that I admired from afar. I liked him but he was distant with me in public.

Not so that night. He was showering me with attention of the kind I liked. He was making suggestive remarks that were working on me. He said, "If you were a girl I would kiss you on the mouth, right now." He was flirting, if a 14-year-old could be capable of that. The opportunity to get physical with Alan Soriano was a fantasy I'd never dreamed of. My little junk was very excited about his interest. I was 12 and in the very early stages of understanding why boys play with their dicks. I hadn't been masturbating for long at that point. But I was a good Catholic boy. I was feeling torn about it. I *wanted* to, badly, but was thrashing about inside over the fact that it was sinful and wrong. I had been taught that having sex with anyone, much less another boy, is a mortal sin. In Catholicism, a mortal sin is the religious equivalent to a Felony. It was serious and you could be sentenced to hell for it.

He had finally talked me into jacking him off. Frankly, it didn't take that much. He led me to the very end of the dorm where we could be alone, and he showed me what he wanted me to do. I was all ears. Of course, it was nothing new to me. We sat down on the edge of someone's bed, and I took his dick in my hand and did what I had always done to Bob Logan, only this time, I was a willing volunteer.

I hadn't noticed, but as we were having our fun, a small group of other cadets, maybe 3 or 4, quietly began to gather, under beds or behind lockers, to watch us. The few other kids who were in the dorm at the time, were asleep and some were on leave with family or friends. It was probably a holiday. I was committed to what I was doing, so I didn't mind them seeing it very much. I just focused on what I was doing. Soriano was enjoying himself and that mattered a great deal to me. I was too.

Suddenly, Soriano's dick erupted, and he stood up laughing and backed away from me as if to run away. He only took a few steps though, because he saw his seed on my hand and was maybe a little proud of himself. I stood up and chased him to wipe the seed on his pajama sleeve. It was all in good fun.

The next day, all of the fun and enjoyment came to a screeching halt. One of our spectators had evidently told someone about what we had done, and word had gotten to Mr. Longo. It wasn't long before everyone knew, fellow cadets and nuns alike. It sent me, and I suspect, Soriano as well, into self-flagellating shame over what had been so fun and exciting just last night. Wow, that was an awfully fast 180-degree turn-a-round.

There was a classroom next door to the one we were so familiar with, that was not being used just then. He ordered Soriano and me into the room and closed the door behind him. He stood in the hallway watching us through the window in the classroom door. He was hoping that we would start having sex.

Soriano mentioned that he thought that's what Mr. Longo was up to, and he was pretty upset about it. He kept looking over at Mr. Longo, angrily, while we talked. Our conversation was tense, frightened and remorseful. He begged me not to say anything. "We can't do that anymore, it's a mortal sin!" he said. We both felt intense shame. What I didn't realize until that moment, was that Soriano was trying to be a good Catholic boy too and was feeling just like I was. There was some meager comfort in knowing that we were having this terrible experience, but we were going through it together. We vowed never to do it again.

Failing to get Soriano and me to get busy in front of him, Mr. Longo then sent me back to class, which was now being supervised by Gary Holly, of all people. Holly was a short almost chubby Asian kid whose continence was the living image of a street urchin. Rough around more than just the edges, he seemed like a kid right out of a Dickens novel. That left Soriano and Mr. Longo alone in the other classroom.

When Mr. Longo brought Soriano back to class, Soriano was visibly angry and embarrassed. Mr. Longo then ordered me into the empty classroom with him. His tone was not his usual contempt. Now, we were friends. He was focused on me and seemed genuinely interested in what I might have to say. He began questioning me about details. He asked me to describe Soriano's dick. "Was it big?" "Did he stick it into my butt?" "Did I put my mouth on it?" "What did Soriano do to me?", "When he came, did it shoot out or ooze?", "Was it a lot, or a little bit?" Mr. Longo wanted to know all the minute details.

Then, to my absolute horror, he asked me to show him what I did with Soriano. He asked me to pull his pants down and do to him what I did to Soriano. He wanted to know the step-by-step details of what we did. He was licking his lips and his vibe was creepy. In Hindsight, he was grooming me. I wouldn't do it despite his persistent encouragement. He had already established himself as an adult who was not on my side. He finally gave up with a sigh of disgust and frustration and sent me back to class.

Thereafter, of course, he resumed his usual posture of disdain and contempt for me as if nothing had happened to alter it. We weren't friends anymore. I was angry, embarrassed and humiliated, much like Soriano was when he returned from *his* talk with Mr. Longo.

Back then things like this was something that kids like me simply had to get used to. It was where we lived. It was a lot like The Scarlet Letter. We were marked and the mark stung with a bitterness for the longest time. Soriano and I were cool though. Well, at least when there was no one else around. After all, he was one of the cool kids and had a reputation to uphold.

In public, it was back to business as usual. Soriano couldn't be seen chumming around with the likes of me. We did interact from time to time after that, but when it was just the two of us, he was always friendly and kind to me. He liked me but couldn't let on when others were around. In public, he was pretty cruel, much like the other Alpha Boys!

There was one younger boy who must have been in another division at St Francis, who ended up at BoysTown during the time I lived there. I didn't know him back then, but he reported that Mr. Longo would have sex parties with a select few of the boys at St Francis, one of which was him.

***

Marching in formation was a big thing for us at St Francis. It was the Academy's way of getting us from one place to another in an orderly manner and teaching us gentlemanly behavior. Each of the sisters had one of those hand-held school bells like the ones teachers used to call kids in from recess back in the day. The nuns would ring theirs when it was time to fall in to go somewhere. We needed to fall in line several times a day and it seemed like every time we were called to fall in, it would be accompanied by prayers or devotional singing.

We would come from the dorm on the 5th floor to the playroom, in the basement. Then from the playroom to school on the third floor. From school to the dining room etc.

At the end of our day, we would make the trek back to the dorm and that was the trip during which I would usually embarrass myself having fantasies about being a queen or a starlet waving to my imaginary adoring public. At times, I was so focused on the fantasy that I would physically act it out. In hindsight, I may have been bringing some of my classmate's jeering on myself with how I acted.

Ingrained in my mind forever will be the sound of all our feet hitting the terrazzo floors in unison, or some version of it. We had spit-shined standard military leather dress shoes; all of us. We had to shine them every night right before taking our daily shower and going to bed.

What was so interesting to me, was the bonding that would happen while we were shining our shoes. Only a very few of us wanted to be there shining our shoes, but we all had to, anyway. Some cadets took no small amount of pride in making those shoes shine to the point there you could see your reflection. I was never that meticulous.

A good clean shoe was all that was expected. We were not permitted to use "Clip-on Ties" either. Double Windsor knot on a navy-blue tie, do or die. Our shoes, along with the backs of our hands, the soles of our feet and behind our ears, were inspected after our shower, before we were allowed put on our pajamas and go to bed.

***

Mike Morrison was another character that would pal around with Matsco, Tobias and me. Also contributing to Morrison being included in our little group was the fact that he and I were in the same class at another Catholic Military academy called "Hall of the Divine Child", in Monroe, several years before.

Morrison was an average boy with dark hair. He had a rigid, very button downed demeanor. Communication with him was always curt and businesslike even when we were relaxing. His resting pulse was one of deep frustration. Clutching with all his might at his father's approval while somehow knowing he could ever be enough to be welcomed back into a family that had since evaporated. Much like mine, come to think of it.

We put up with Morrison's quirkiness because that's just the way he was. Other kids were put off by it and I suppose that's how he ended up in our little group. Our peers showed no mercy in their criticism and ridicule. We were frequently on the losing end of intentional cruelty.

The cool kids had the ability to ferret out any little flaw or action in one another and blow it up into a full-blown identity. Like "Honey". That was my nickname at St. Francis. It was given to me by Mr. Longo, who said it with a tone positively dripping with contempt. The nickname caught on with most of my classmates, so that was my nickname from then on.

The other nickname I had for a short while was "Pussy Galore" after the character in the James Bond movie "Goldfinger". The nuns had to put the kibosh on that one shortly after hearing it crop up. This was, after all, a Catholic Military Academy. There are proprieties that go along with running a Catholic School and "Pussy Galore" was certainly not among them.

The year Morrison and I were on the rifle exhibition team together, St Francis Academy was offering a medal for the best rifle exhibition cadet. All of us were required to compete if we wanted to remain on the squad. I was one of them.

***

I am usually a mess under pressure, and I was never one to enjoy competitions. I much preferred teamwork and common goals. I could easily hide in that environment. That was the basis on which the Rifle Exhibition Team usually operated. On the drill team we all had to depend on one another to be where we were supposed to be at the exact second, we were supposed to be there, to catch an airborne rifle or to keep our marching formations visibly sharp.

It was a sudden death competition! Mr. Longo ordered all of us to one end of the gym in formation and ran us through our drills. Some of the drills were kind of tricky and required a lot of memorization. They're called "Manuals" and each one had a succession of steps you had to do, in a specific order. Altogether, I can't recall how many manuals we had been trained to do, but there were a lot of them. We had to keep all of them straight in our heads.

There were Standard Manuals and Parade Manuals numbering from 3 to 21. Once, during our training, we were taken to the Light Guard Armory on a field trip. The senior ROTC guys, the ones in college ROTC, were doing manuals that lasted as long as 10 minutes. They included a lot of complicated choreography, and it was really quite something to watch.

We young cadets had grown to think we were hot stuff, but these guys were on a whole other level. It kind of put us in our place to see what the big boys could do. The next time we assembled in the gym, back home, we were not nearly so cocky. Mr. Longo's field trip to the armory had accomplished its mission. Our attention was now focused. In order to do this right, like the big guys do, we had a *lot* of work ahead of us.

Mr. Longo started with the short ones like the 3 and 5 count manuals and worked his way up to the big one. To us, that was the 21 Count Parade Manual, which included flipping the rifle in mid air, a specific number of rotations, and catching it on its way down, along with a bunch of other movements. He would give a command and when someone screwed up, he would call out their name and order them to "Fall Out".

By the time we got to the 16-count parade manual there were only 4 of us left. Morrison and I were two of them. Surprisingly, Reynolds was not left standing, which was terrifying to me, because he was our platoon leader, our golden child. I would never have imagined that I would still be standing after he was eliminated.

As we waited for the next command, we each took a sideways glance at each other. I was smiling because I was so excited. I would never have dared hope that I'd get this far. Everybody knew I was a dip-shit and it just wasn't like me to do all that without screwing anything up. By this time, the entire squad was milling around watching Me & Morrison, after being eliminated.

We were finally at the big 21 Count Parade Manual and me and Morrison were the only two still standing. The reaction from the room was the same disbelief that I was feeling. In stark contrast, I felt Morrison's nervousness like a cold breeze rushing past me as we stood at attention waiting for the command.

Still shaking his head in amazement, Mr. Longo ordered us to stand back-to-back so we couldn't see one another and began the count. "1, 2, 3, 4, 5, 6, 7, 8, 9, 10, 11, 12 Morrison, Fall Out" he barked and resumed counting. "13, 14, 15, 16, 17, 18, 19, 20, 21.

"Well, I'll be dipped in shit, Honey, you did it!" Mr. Longo spat. "If I hadn't seen it with my own eyes, I'd never believe it." The others were shocked as well, and some even congratulated me.

In my head, I was the king of the world, at least for the moment. My Bar (medal) hadn't arrived yet, but it was going to be lonely on my chest. When I graduated, I think I had maybe 3 bars to my dress uniform. One of which everyone had, just for being on the squad.

For weeks after that win, I was just about unbearable to anyone who got near me, including the nuns. I was a snotty little twit, to be honest. I had finally attained something good and was milking it for all it was worth.

Sister Mary Lucille got so sick of my attitude, one afternoon, that she threatened to take my bar away. I looked her straight in the eye and said, "You can't take it away because I already earned it. It's mine and you can't do anything about it!"

That was uncharacteristic of me to be that boldly insubordinate. Frankly, the fact that she didn't give me a sound smack right there where I stood is a testament to her restraint and decorum.

"Alright, Mr. Smarty-Pants, that does it!" she barked. "In the Playroom right now", she hissed as she grabbed my arm and led me through the janitor room, past the property cage, to her desk in the playroom.

Sister Lucille looked almost Asian with her dark features and steely black eyes. Acne had obviously ravaged her otherwise lovely face when she was a teenager. She was barely taller than we were and talked in stern tones through her teeth as if her jaw had been wired so she couldn't open her mouth all the way when she talked. It was even more pronounced when she was angry, like she was with me all too often. Like today, for example.

She could ordinarily strike fear into my very soul with a stern look, but today I was certain that she was morally wrong, and I was willing to march into hell rather than let her get away with it. So, into hell I marched with a firm and deliberate stride.

***

There was an incident about a year before when she was really, *really* mad at me, even more than she was today. She took me into a then empty kitchen and accused me of lying to her about the fact that I had run away the night before and got back before the wake-up bell. I continued to lie, and this set her off like I had never seen before. She grabbed me by my tie and a handful of my shirt and lifted me up and slammed me against a refrigerator and held me there. She cocked her arm back and made a fist aimed at my face. I was in terror!

She didn't complete the punch because I began singing for my life. I told her everything. She cautioned me to never lie to her again. She demanded my demerit card and angrily marked the living daylights out of it. I had no reference point at the time, but I didn't realize that I was dealing with a woman of color who grew up on the streets of Detroit in the 50s. This was no delicate little flower we were dealing with, here. She was not about to be trifled with by the likes of a snotty little 13-year-old dweeb like me.

***

Sister Lucille unlocked the game closet behind her desk and withdrew a paddle that was longer and a little wider than the one she usually used. "Corporal Punishment" is what Catholics call getting a spanking. It didn't require much of an offense, and always happened in public as an example to the others. This time, however, Sister Lucille and I were alone.

The Paddle she brought out had marks or inscriptions on it, no doubt the names of some of the more notable students who had survived its powerful sting. Maybe they were notches like on a gunslinger's belt. I didn't pay enough attention to it to see for sure what the inscriptions might have been. I had other things on my mind. She turned to me and stood there holding the paddle for a moment, visibly continuing to calm herself. She had been shaking with anger while she brought me inside.

She took a deep breath and began to speak. "Schroeder" she said, "I know that this bar means a lot to you and maybe you have worked hard to earn it. I don't know. But that does not give you the right to be insubordinate to your superiors." As she was speaking, she continued to calm herself. She seemed to become more rational and collected with each sentence.

"I guess I'm not going to take your precious bar away, but as long as I'm the prefect in this division, you will speak to your superiors with respect, or you will hear from me" she said. I breathed a sigh of relief and vindication. She wasn't going to take my bar away and, for me, that was the whole issue.

By this time, she was her usual cool, calm and collected self and she motioned me to bend over and put my hands on the desk like I had done so many times before and seen so many others be ordered to do. Her tone was almost kind as she ordered me into position for what was to come. I leaned over and put my hands on the desk for support and waited motionless.

I was calm too. I didn't feel so frustrated now. She had acknowledged that she was wrong to threaten me in that way, so I was willing to quietly resign myself to cooperate with what we both knew had to be done.

"Whack" went the paddle, just once. I could tell her heart wasn't really in it. I imagined that the paddle would have stung a lot more if she'd wanted it to. Either that, or the paddle was designed for psychological impact rather than function. But, as it was, it was almost painless. I silently waited for the next whack. But it did not come.

After a long pause, "Schroeder" she said, "Let this be a lesson to you. Don't ever speak to a superior like that again." I stood up and we looked at one another for a beat and she acquiescently sighed, "You're dismissed." I thanked her and made my hasty retreat out to the playground. Sister Lucille remained behind seeming to be deep in thought.

CHAPTER 16

A Good Catholic Boy

I have what can only be described as a "complicated" relationship with The Holy Catholic Church. In all the ways that matter, I was raised by the Catholic Church. The Priests, Nuns and Brothers ended up being my parents. I was born in a Catholic Hospital and almost all of my education was in Catholic Schools, three of which I lived in. I was baptized in a Catholic Children's Home and my adoption into the Schroeder family was handled by Catholic Social Services in Detroit and when my brother and I became wards of the court of St Clair County, Catholic Social Services was appointed to over-see my care. My confirmation was at St. Francis.

Confirmation to a Catholic boy is kind of like a Bar Mitzvah is to a Jewish boy, both happen at the same general time in a boy's life. In the Catholic Church, when you are confirmed, you are required to select a Catholic Saint as your Patron. That would be the Saint that you would be expected to model your life after. I chose St. Casimir because I thought Casey would be a cool name to have. I had to look him up, just now, because I had no idea what he was supposed to be the patron saint of. I just thought the name was cool.

It turns out that he is the Patron Saint of Lithuania and died in 1484 at the age of 23 or 25 depending on which account you read. The rest is also pretty sketchy, but he was a prince in the royal family of Poland and most of what he was famous for happened after he had already died. There are mentions of failed military conquests, music and diplomacy in his history. He wasn't exactly a famous Saint, like St Francis of Assisi, St. Peter or Saint Christopher. I guess you could call him a "C-List" Saint. You need to do a little digging to find him.

The Catholic Church didn't accept gay people back then. To be fair, in recent years, the church has put up some window dressing of acceptance, but not so far as to allow homosexuals to participate in Catholic Sacraments. I learned that in my brief dalliance with "Dignity" (Gay Catholics) as an adult. My dalliance was brief because we weren't allowed to worship in the sanctuary where the other Catholics worshiped. We were relegated to the basement and a member of the catholic clergy couldn't be present. We were left to "Pretend" on our own. I found that offensive to the point of being kinky and I left, post haste. I simply couldn't understand how a person could be devoted to a religion that doesn't accept them; a religion that condemns such people to an eternity in hell.

I did graduate at BoysTown, as expected and immediately tried to divorce the church. In all honesty, I tried to divorce the Catholic Church while I was still in high school. But Fr. Farald's uncharacteristically vehement response to that idea quickly slammed the brakes on the very idea.

I did not set foot in a Catholic Church for more than two decades after I graduated from High School. My strategy was to miss my Easter Duties enough times that I would be excommunicated without having to burn in hell for eternity.

That didn't work as the Catholic Church was, then, well into the process of adjusting to the times. First, it was celebrating Mass in English instead of the traditional Latin. When I was first made aware that I was a Catholic, Mass was all done in Latin. Precious few Catholics had any knowledge of what was being said at Mass. Then it was no longer a sin to eat meat on Friday. It had been a venial sin. A venial sin was something like a traffic infraction. It won't get you thrown in hell, but it's a little bit of a swerve from adherence to the canon. An un-repented venial sin will send you to purgatory, when you die, where you would languish for a while before being admitted into the actual heaven. I don't recall any guidance about how long sentences to purgatory would last, or for which venial sins that had not been confessed and expunged from your record.

As time went by, other requirements to being a Catholic were loosened until today. Now a person can be a serial killer/rapist, sitting on death row, having never set foot in a Catholic Church since childhood, and still, legally, be a Catholic. Of course, you *can* molest as many children as you want, but you still can't be gay. There's no longer a way out short of denouncing the church. That, my dear reader, *will* get you condemned to hell. But remember, I'm gay so I'm going there anyway.

That brings me to the complicated relationship I have with The Holy Catholic Church today. For my whole life, there was always plenty of food to eat, medical, dental and vision care when needed, an excellent education, and a roof over my head. More often than not, what's under those Catholic roofs was nothing short of opulent accommodations. I am grateful for all of that. I never would have made it this far without Catholics. There was always love of a sort. A love borne of pity and duty and service to humanity, but no less in earnest. The Catholic Church is, in any real sense, my parents.

At the same time, under those same Catholic roofs, I had suffered a great deal physically, mentally and psychologically, not the least of which was me being gay in environments that didn't respect, or even grudgingly accept, my humanity. I was always a problem to be solved, not because I was a bad person or prone to destructive or aggressive behavior, but because of who I am. How does one "Walk that off?" I'm just another, among millions of men who are mad at their parents, while dying inside for their approval.

There is no doubt that this has had a lifelong negative impact on my growth and development. I have little to suggest that said impact will ever change. It is an intrinsic part of who I am now. That's how I've always been seen by my "Parents", teachers, "Siblings" and society in general. An Outcast! I have The Holy Catholic Church to thank for all of that, as well. I still want a divorce. An emancipation, if you will, that may never come. That's my spectrum.

I had been well trained, some might say indoctrinated, that God never leaves you, no matter what. I found that attractive. I really needed something, or anything really, that would not abandon me again. By this time, I had learned well that I was an inconvenience; an anomaly.

Everywhere I had lived since that day outside the courtroom was a "Temporary solution until a more permanent arrangement could be found." I was now 13 years old and had no hard evidence that such a place even existed. None of the kids I grew up with could report that they had ever seen such a place, yet each of them, could testify that said mythical place was what was being planned for them, as well.

I leaned to God a lot, growing up, because of that teaching. I had nurtured a faith that a permanent home *would* be found for me. It's true that God never does abandon anyone. After all, God is our own creation and has no control over us to begin with. We are, in a very real sense, in control of wherever God is, or isn't in our lives. To the extent that we decide where God is in our lives, that is where God will always be. There must be at least some comfort in knowing that God can't get lost. He will always be right there where we last left him.

I had been well trained to be a good Catholic Boy. St. Francis was part of that training. I had plenty of reference points on how to do that, and even more points on how *not* to. I wanted to be a good Catholic Boy who, not only does what he is told, but is liked by superiors and peers alike and is found to be "Worthy in the eyes of God."

I am convinced that in the Catholic traditional way of thinking, "Worthy in the eyes of God" was not possible for a young boy in The US in the 50s and 60s, least of all, a decidedly odd and gay one like me. I spent a great deal of time trying anyway. I was never without support from superiors while making my attempts, either. I was an altar boy, and a commentator while at St Francis. The Commentator was the term used at the time for whoever is reading the scriptures to the congregation that would be talked about in the sermon. I loved the attention and the responsibility placed in me, to be selected to do it to begin with.

At St. Francis there were never Bibles about. Bible scriptures were always in the form of missals; books that contained some scriptures, but always with the Catholic interpretation of what they mean. The artwork in those missals was superb and engaging. I still think so.

The fact that I was trying to be "Worthy in the Eyes of God", seemed to weigh in decisions about how much trouble I was in when I was in trouble. Saying rosaries with Sister Mary Frances before going to bed was working for me too. Sister Frances would say a rosary every night before lights out and any cadet was welcome to join her, but that much was voluntary. I had a beautiful rosary that someone had given me, and I wore a scapular and a St. Christopher medal under my shirt every day. At least part of me was always deeply sincere about all this, but I could never get past my additional motives. Looking the part of a Good Catholic Boy was also doing wonders for me in the real world.

I was Gay, and almost everyone around me knew it but me. I probably did know, but I wouldn't call it that and I certainly wasn't in a position where I could accept it if I *did*. At a number of places where I lived, The Church would encouraged me to seek a vocation to the priesthood or brotherhood. Subtly, and sometimes not so subtly, all effeminate boys were so encouraged.

I can't confirm my suspicion that the Catholic Church was doing this to everyone who acted "swishy" like me, but it had always looked like it. The logic was that if a gay boy or girl were to be ordained, they would have to take a vow of celibacy and that would dispense with the whole messy subject of homosexuality. "What do you suppose they were thinking?" I thought. "No Sex=No Gay?"

Given that that was the standard operational procedure at the time, it doesn't seem like Rocket Science to figure out why The Holy Catholic Church is in so much trouble today. When you try to suppress something as intrinsic to being human as a person's sexuality, it's going to find it's way out, one way or another. When appropriate avenues are blocked, it will have no choice but to come out in inappropriate ways. That's just how it works!

CHAPTER 17

BoysTown Freshman Year

According to records that I obtained a few decades later, my fate as I graduated from 8th Grade came down to this. If "Fr Flanagan's BoysTown" wouldn't accept me, I would be committed to a mental institution. I was to graduate from 8th grade shortly and there was apparently no place else in Michigan to put me. At that point BoysTown was roughly 50 years old and getting accepted was no small feat. The school had a well-deserved reputation as a prep school version of an Ivy League college.

Here's the entirety of a psych evaluation I found in my Catholic Social Services record that was done when I was 11. This was after my time with the Schmidts:

> (sic)"During the interview, Dr. Locket found Greg to have average or better intelligence; to be proper and distant but cooperative; he showed little anxiety. He uses extremely strong defenses of: denial, intellectualization and rationalization. Denial is mostly on the conscious level and may be a denial of being male on the subconscious level. This denial started early, thus forming a personality pattern of which his overt feminine character pattern is only a part.
>
> Dr Locket suggested that initial rejection led to lack of involvement with others for which Greg developed a survival pattern. Greg has a basic personality problem in relating to others. Although it's not definitely known, one could say that

there's a distortion in Greg's relationship to his mother and a lack of involvement with his father. Greg relates on a superficial level and one wonders what he really feels.

Dr Locket diagnosed him as having a passive, receptive, feminine personality pattern. He further described Greg as being; narcissistic (involved more with self than with others); masochistic (as evidence in his passivity in the face of scapegoating); relatively un-relating, unmotivated and markedly defensive. He probably has overwhelming anger, but good defenses.

Greg's future depends on how much anxiety can be aroused. As he becomes older he may become anxious and do something. Dr. Locket recommended long term placement in a total care environment for all his childhood."

I include it for two reasons. One, to show what the psychological community thought of homosexuality at the time. But also because it demonstrates the extent of trauma. I *was* pretty messed up.

***

As luck, or Mrs. Herzog's skill, would have it, BoysTown did say "Yes". I was to board a plane and fly off to Omaha where I would be met by someone From BoysTown to begin my new life. It was the first time I had ever flown, and the romance and excitement of the flight kept any feelings of loneliness and abandonment at bay. For the time being, that would have to wait. I was too excited.

It's probably important to interject, here, that it's 1966 and I'm 14 at this point. My hormones are beginning to rage just like anyone else at that age. I had already had sexual encounters including an abusive relationship with an older boy. It's gradually becoming clear that I like boys, but I'm not allowed to because I'm a Catholic. These priests, brothers and nuns were my parents, for heaven's sake. When I would try to talk to any of them about what was happening inside me, the response would always be the same as if it were written in a protocol manual that they all were reading from. There's something wrong with you. You have to stop this. Your only option is to Pray the Gay Away. It's no wonder gay kids feel so alone. You can see where the problem is.

***

This might be a good time to take a break and talk about the internal struggle that gay people go through growing up. Gay people are no different than straight people when it comes to biology. Hormones will rage at that age and if everything you've ever been taught says that you are not allowed to do *anything* about it except pray away the gay, it doesn't take much to figure out that there's going to be some internal turmoil.

Your biology, your mind and your spirit are all pulling at you in different directions and it's constant. It just goes on and on and it never stops. You get moments now and then when you feel calm for an hour or so, but mostly, it never stops. It's relentless! Day after day and night after night, always thinking, always thrashing, always fighting. Always so vigilant and so careful to make sure nobody finds out while you sneak a peek at that compellingly beautiful classmate and then self flagellate about it, thinking that you're trash for doing it, and heaven forbid that you should get caught by the object of your desire. It could mean that you might get a sound ass whooping to top off your deep shame. That's what I mean when I tell you that my high school years were fraught with anxiety and restraint. I think most people would call that torture.

At BoysTown it was assumed that everyone was straight, and the staff treated us accordingly. At the time, the Catholic Church did not recognize homosexuality as a thing someone could be. To the Church, a gay person was a heterosexual that was morally weak, and we were taught, and were expected to, struggle against these urges that happen to all human beings at that age. They called it "Unnatural" they called it "Perverse". And if we failed to stop it from happening then we were lacking in strength, We were morally weak. It was our own fault because we weren't making the cut to be worthy in the eyes of God. We were "Less Than".

Being a good Catholic boy and having The Catholic Church as my parents, I assumed that they were correct and so that's how I treated my "Perversion", my "Sickness". I was doing my best to play the role of being straight, but I was understandably bad at it. Everything in my world was resolute that there was something wrong with me and that it was no *little* thing.

Of course, there *was* something wrong with me and it *was* no little thing, but it had precious little to do with the fact that I was gay. Little did I know that, well intention-ed as they may have been, my "Parents" had been accidentally abusing me this whole time and were continuing to do so; and with *my* cooperation, no less! Surely, they didn't know that they were hurting me.

***

When new boys arrive at BoysTown they go through Orientation to get acclimated to their new environment. It was a lot to take in. Everything had procedures and protocols that we would learn along the way from staff and fellow students alike. For example, we didn't do "Chores" we did "Charges" and there were a hundred little things like that that we had to learn. Some of it was familiar to me having spent time in Catholic Military Schools before. In fact, I was coming from one when I arrived at BoysTown. BoysTown is not a military academy, but there is quite a bit of overlap between the two.

In Orientation, we stayed in a nice apartment and there were 5 of us. There would be an Orientation Counselor with us 24/7, so there were three shifts when I was there. We were gradually introduced to the Dining Halls, School, Church, and recreation. It took a week or so. We would be shuffled off to different locations around campus learning how BoysTown works.

BoysTown is a city in every sense of the word. It has its own US Post Office, Schools, a Theater, a medical center, Churches, a working farm, a Field House complete with an Olympic sized swimming pool. It had tennis and handball courts too. I guess you'd have to call it a sports complex. BoysTown even has its own man-made lake. There were no fences around BoysTown. There was nothing preventing anyone from leaving. I don't even know that there was ever a security force at all. There was a guy who would be driving around in a truck at different times, but I think he was more grounds maintenance than anything.

***

I didn't cry myself to sleep my first night in BoysTown. That wasn't like me. This time it was different. Although I was just over 700 miles from anything I knew yesterday, maybe I had finally grown somewhat accustomed to being uprooted and displaced so often. Up to this point, that had been, roughly, an annual event since I was 4.

At BoysTown there was no talk of adoption or a new placement with a foster family being planned. No dangling carrots in this new world. Those days were over. I could feel it because no one was suggesting anything different. This was it. For what it's worth, this was my home now!

During Orientation, every boy was screened for one of the Choirs. It wasn't a voluntary thing, either. We all had to audition, like it or not. There were choirs at BoysTown, and they were important.

To my chagrin, I failed my audition miserably. The audition didn't take long. I was able to frustrate this poor priest in a matter of minutes. His devotion to music, in a very Catholic kind of way, was plainly visible. Reverent and passionate as if music was how you struggle and suffer to become worthy in the eyes of God. Struggle and suffering on our path to finding God are very Catholic ideals. It's in our DNA. I must have seemed pitiful to this poor fellow, a veritable insult to music.

It didn't take long for me to become interested in things to keep my mind off my circumstances. This was a Catholic School, after all. Catholics are not playing around when it comes to education. There were plenty of challenges, some of which I was able to meet, albeit with my face pressed back. By this point, staff at BoysTown had spent 5 decades developing a strong set of programs to keep us busy and by the time I arrived, they had gotten awfully good at it!

I was curious to meet Fr Flanagan and asked about him as soon as we rose the next day. I had seen the movie with Spencer Tracy and Mickey Rooney, and I was dying to meet him. Maybe, I could even get a piece of candy from him like Mickey Rooney does in the movie. I was ceremoniously escorted to a big cathedral looking church and directed to an iron gate beyond which was an ornate mausoleum. My escort pointed to it and whispered with a smile, "He's been dead for 22 years!" I know that was a little dig at my innocent ignorance of the history of BoysTown, but I thought it kind of funny.

From Orientation I moved to Marquette Hall. I was assigned to "Upper Left". It was a grand and collegiate looking 2 story Tudor Mansion having 4 big apartments housing 20 boys in each. Marquette Hall was on the grade school side of the town, just across a courtyard from Ryan Hall. The two were where High School Freshmen lived, almost like a second orientation before moving to "The High School Side" as we enter our sophomore year. We went to school on "the high school side" but lived on "the grade school side". Church was smack dab between them like a sentinel guarding over the two.

CHAPTER 17

There were two dining halls: one for grade school and another for high school. There were protocols for that too, just like everything else. We would arrive on a strict timeline and stand behind our chair to wait until prayers were done and then sit down to eat. The food would already be on the table, and we had 15 minutes to eat it. When the bell rang, it was time to leave whether you had finished your meal or not. Some of the boys, whose job it was, would stay behind to start the clean-up as we were still leaving the hall. It was like a well-oiled machine, the way it worked.

I don't recall ever being hungry at BoysTown, but by the same token, I don't recall any particularly memorable meals while I lived there. This was industrial cooking. Feeding hundreds of people at once limits the possibility of gourmet meals.

Not that the food was terrible, it just wasn't anything I'd feel a need to write home about. If I had one, that is. I remember being served chipped beef on toast. In the military they call it "Shit on a Shingle" and I liked it. Having had that meal served at military schools before, it was nothing new to me. I also recall being served what BoysTown called "Pizza". I'd had pizza before, many times. You can't fool me; this was not pizza! I'm not entirely sure what you'd call it, but it was tasty and sufficiently filling. I looked forward to it just like everyone else did. To their credit, neither dinning hall ever once tried to feed me liver and for that, I offer my sincere gratitude to those hard-working cooks.

***

Our Church was called the Dowd Chapel. To call it a chapel was an understatement, at the very least. It was the kind of old school cathedral you'd expect to see in Europe somewhere. There was lots of marble, arches, terrazzo and dark wood. It seated every student at BoysTown, and most of the staff, all at once. The Theater could fit all of us too. They called it The Auditorium. That's where school assemblies were held. Except at Christmas time. Then it magically becomes "The Boar's Head Inn", where we would see movies on each of the 12 nights of Christmas, if we wanted. Of course, we couldn't take food or drink in there. The floor was carpeted. There wasn't even a concessions stand in the entire building.

Christmas at BoysTown was always a big deal! Staff pulled out all the stops to make it as nice and festive as they could while respecting that most of us who remained at BoysTown during the Holidays were kind of sad about it. Most of the rules were suspended and those of us left behind could do, or not do, whatever we wanted, within reason.

Close to half of the boys would be gone, visiting with Family or whatever they had before they were accepted to BoysTown. I was always left behind because I didn't have a family or a home other than BoysTown to go to. The Holidays were that time of year when the fact that I was alone in the world would be right up in my face. It was always a sad time for me, a constant reminder that I was unwanted. Even now, I dread the Holidays because it's a loud and present reminder of what I *didn't* have growing up. That can't be blamed on BoysTown, though, the staff made a genuine effort every year.

There would be lots of presents at Christmas time. Some were from student's families and others were from the public at large. BoysTown had a good reach into communities and there would be a flood of donations of Christmas gifts that might be of interest to young boys. Kind of like a Toy Drive. Counselors would, of course, know which boys didn't have families and the donated gifts would be distributed among them. Most of the time, the gifts would be generic in nature. Things like model planes, cologne sets, toiletries, clothes and food or candy. But everyone got presents for Christmas every year without fail!

***

Everyone at BoysTown had an after-school job to earn our

allowance. It was 50 cents a week, as I recall. It wasn't money, it was a kind of script that you could only spend at BoysTown. We had a canteen with a bowling alley and lunch counter where we could spend our allowance on stuff like candy, cigarettes, records, ice cream, junk food and maybe a burger at the lunch counter.

Yes, I said Cigarettes. This was 1966 and everybody still smoked; teachers, counselors, everybody. You could smoke on buses and airplanes and in restaurants; pretty much anywhere you wanted. The laws didn't even *start* changing until the early 70s

Piotrosky had gotten me into smoking while I was still at Marquette Hall. We weren't allowed to smoke as Freshmen living on the grade school side. "Pio", as we called him, always had some smokes and didn't like smoking alone. He had developed a way to light them that he must have learned from someone who had been in prison. He would take some steel wool we used during "Charges" and fashion it into a horseshoe shape and stick both ends into the slots of an electrical outlet. It would immediately turn red, and we would light our cigarettes on it. We were rebels without a clue.

***

My after-school job at BoysTown was as a library assistant. Our librarian was Mrs. Lystra Kinkner, ably assisted by Mr. Wilhelm Wehbey, who was also our speech coach. I knew way more about the Dewey Decimal System than a civilian ought to know.

I loved Mr. Wehbey. He was my primary Father Figure at BoysTown. He looked like he might have been Arabic with his dark features and slick jet-black hair. It was the age of Pomade and Brylcreem. They would give it to us at BoysTown for free, attempting to keep us from trying to wear our hair like The Beatles. Short back and sides was the expected grooming protocol and there was more than a little resistance to it among my classmates. I can just hear Monsignor Wagner grumbling,

"These kids and their wild, crazy hair, we're going to have to put a stop to that!" Monsignor Nicholas Wagner succeeded Fr Flanagan as the Executive Director of BoysTown.

Mr. Wehbey's first language was German, but he spoke English with barely a hint of an accent. His right arm had been injured in the war which kept his arm stationary at a mild angle like you see male models in magazines do as a standard pose. The injury, whatever it may have been, did not stop Mr. Wehbey from being able to play his guitar. The angle in his arm just happened to be perfect for his picking hand. He played flamenco music with what, to me, was passion and precision. He didn't do it often, but it was fascinating to watch and hear. His guitar playing was how I learned about Django Reinheart. I had asked him one time if it was hard to play with his injury, and all. That's when Mr. Wehbey told me about Django Rienhardt and what he had to overcome to write and perform the guitar pieces that made him famous. "This is nothing compared to what he had to go through." he said.

There was something a little bit dark about Mr. Wehbey; something lurking in the shadows. I always assumed it was trauma from the war. He was a bit of a tortured soul. It wasn't a subtle vibe, either. You could see that he was struggling inside. He wasn't very good at hiding it. It didn't seem to affect his kindness, though. I learned shortly after graduating that Mr. Wehbey ended his own life a few years later. Although I was saddened by the news, I was not surprised.

Lystra Kinkner was another character altogether; almost cartoon-ish. She carried herself with a straight up Grandmotherly vibe. She was always active and sharp as a tack. She was ready to laugh at any moment and her laughter was a beautiful sound. Her strong but high-pitched voice made me think that maybe she had been a singer in her younger years. There was a musical sing-song quality to how she spoke. She dressed and groomed like a woman from the past. Always clean

CHAPTER 17

and presentable.

Once Mrs. Kinkner got to know me a little, she would suggest books for me to read. She introduced me to James Thurber, Moss Hart, Walter Mitty, Henry David Thoreau and Allen Drury. Yeah, I think she knew I was gay! By the time I got to BoysTown I'm pretty sure I had already read every Nancy Drew Mystery that had been printed to date. The Library at BoysTown didn't have any Nancy Drew Mysteries. They had The Hardy Boys. I tried to slog my way through one of them,, once but it just made me miss Nancy Drew.

I wasn't a big reader at BoysTown like I was at the Schmidt's Farm. There wasn't nearly the free time, but Mrs. Kinkner's suggestions did spark my interest. Most of my reading was taken up by studying for debate and Model UN. It was mostly Newspapers, The Congressional Record and news magazines like Time, Newsweek and US News & World Report. I was truly engaged by Debate and Model UN.

***

At Marquette Hall on Saturdays when there was some free time, Rasmussen and I would play with music. I had my trusty stereo record player and Rasmussen had a small portable tape recorder. We would record fake interviews with stars by asking a question, on the tape, and then play a snippet of sound from one of the records as the answer, hoping they would be funny. We had to time it just right. It was quite the chore to sync the tape recorder with the record player because that type of sound editing technology had not been invented yet. We did it manually and it took hours to record just a minute or two of Jokes. These tapes were a favorite to the boys in Upper Left and Rasmussen and I thoroughly enjoyed making them. It was engaging, to say the least. An entire day would slip by while we barely even noticed.

I had begun to sense a vibe at my new home. It wasn't spoken, but it was just sort of hanging in the air all the time. It felt like, "Everybody here has a sad story, but that was then, and this is now, Now we're starting over and we're doing it together, this time." There was always something to do and plenty of other boys to do it with. I was at long last, becoming part of a family.

We had to go to Mass a couple times a week and we had to go to confession at some point every week before Mass so we could receive communion. You couldn't receive communion while there was a sin on your soul. You had to confess and repent because you had to be clean and pure inside to receive communion and we had to receive communion twice a week. It wasn't like we could duck out if we had recently sinned. It might be important to note that we were teenage boys and masturbation was a sin. Many a lad, including me, would have to skirt the rules on a relatively regular basis.

Most weeks, I would make up sins I had committed because I was a good Catholic boy and didn't usually have much scandal to report. I would be given a short list of prayers to repeat as my penance and "Presto" I was ready for Mass. I don't recall that anyone had ever checked to make sure I had actually done my penance. There was no protocol for that, but I diligently did mine anyway. I've done a lot of penance for things I didn't do, but it was all part of my training, so I did it. I often wonder how the Catholic Church imagines this would all occur to the mind and heart of a hormonal 14-year-old boy.

While I was still living at Marquette Hall, there was a sex scandal involving some boys from Ryan Hall. It was rumored that 4 boys were removed from BoysTown when one of them contracted Syphilis and while doing epidemiology on him, the three others were discovered, all of whom were found to have had it as well. One of the four was a boy that lived in Upper Left at Marquette Hall, where I lived. That's how I found out about it. I felt sorry for him because he was a nice guy and was our comic relief. He was black and handsome. A dapper fellow, always careful with his grooming and quick with a joke.

***

I was diagnosed with a hydrocele in one testicle, while a freshman, which required surgery. So I spent a few nights at BoysTown's hospital. The surgery actually took place at a hospital in Omaha, but the recovery took place at BoysTown.

The night nurse was Brother Vincent who was short and round and not at all attractive. He reminded me of Peter Lorre's Hunchback of Notre Dame character from the movie of the same name. Not That bad, of course, but you get the picture. There were rumors floating around BoysTown of Brother Vincent molesting boys at night when they were in the Hospital. Some a little more assertively than others, it would seem.

The rumors were true. Brother Vincent woke me up in the middle of the night a few times by playing with my butt one night and with my penis and testicles on another. In all fairness, my recovery was from surgery on one of my testicles and a case could be made that he might have had reason to briefly observe my privates, but that's not what it felt like while it was happening. I was being molested.

I didn't report the incident for two reasons. The rumors were widespread enough that everyone already knew, and secondly, I stopped him before he got into anything more than a little bit of touching. The stories going around were much more extensive than what happened to me. Pedophiles being protected by the Catholic Church were nothing new, even in 1966. Like I said, that was just something kids like me had to deal with. It was a part of growing up in a Catholic institution. It's not like it was happening constantly, everywhere we went, but over time, I just learned how to navigate it when it happened.

***

For most of my freshman year, I was studying and adjusting to a new world. There were some good times and some friendships developed, but mostly more of the same things I experienced in other group living situations. I had a few close friends, and generally tolerated the alpha kids who would routinely chide and bully me and my friends. As freshmen, we would be mildly hazed like you might see at a college fraternity. The hazing was very mild compared to the stories we hear these days. Upper class-men were the elite and we were just plebes working toward the day we would eventually replace them in the pecking order. There was a very prominent Catholic Collegiate feel to the social environment at BoysTown. Our lives were socially, intellectually and spiritually geared toward college, followed by a life of relative wealth. It was expected of us.

CHAPTER 18

BoysTown Sophomore Year

When I became a sophomore, I was moved over to Cottage 22 in Section 2 on the High School side. BoysTown is divided about in the middle. One side is the working farm, housing, the school and dining hall for the grade school. The other side is the cottages, the high school, the dining hall, the trade school and the field house.

The "cottages" were Tudor style mansions, much like Marquette, Ryan and Gregory Halls on the Grade School side, but smaller. 5 bedrooms, 4 boys to a room, including an apartment for our cottage counselor along with bigger versions of the standard common areas you find in any normal home. We didn't have kitchens, though. We went to the dinning hall for meals. There are about 5 different designs of these cottages on the High School Side and they were divided into 4 sections with 5 or 6 cottages in each. It was a lot like a modern subdivision. A few designs were randomly repeated throughout.

Section 4 was all Choir Boys. BoysTown was selling records of our Concert Choir at the time. These were the elite Choirboys. They would be touring the world as a kind of ambassadors of goodwill and promotion for BoysTown. There were, 2 other Choirs for different applications. One was the Choir that sang in the Choir Loft in church, several times a week, and a chancel choir. Some of the better, more motivated singers were in more than one of them, too!

I met Danny Presnell in Debate and Model UN. We were

in the same year and had fallen in together like we were actually related. In a sense, we kind of were. He was a slightly chubby fellow with blond hair and piercing light blue eyes. His nickname was "Duck" because that's what he looked like when he walked. It was a kind of comical waddle, and the shape of his body accentuated the image.

He had a younger brother named Ron who was a year behind us at BoysTown. Ron was easily the black sheep of his family. He looked like a younger thinner Danny and ran track throughout high school. Although they were brothers by blood, they didn't seem to like one another very much. I didn't even know the two were related until our junior year.

Danny was a take charge kind of guy around me, deferring only to the coolest black kids among us. There were a lot of them too. Danny just automatically assumed the position of my big brother even though we were the same age. That's how he always treated me. Sometimes I think he was trying to replace Ron in his life, with me. We had no way of knowing it, but my relationship with both brothers would continue well past graduation.

My high school years were primarily occupied with Speech, Debate and Model United Nations. Danny chose the United Arab Republic to represent. My first instinct was to pick The United States as the country I would represent, but Stan Strubble had already picked it, so I had to come up with some other country.

After some historical digging, and a few dropped hints from Mr. Whehbey, I picked Poland. I think he knew me better than I knew myself. It seemed somehow fitting. I had low self-esteem and was often the butt of condescending jokes and being picked on a lot. What cemented my choice was learning that Poland had been completely wiped off the map twice, at that point, and had come back from it both times. That seemed a lot like me.

I represented Poland for the 3 years of High school that Model

UN existed, and by the time I graduated, precious few fellow students were telling "Pollock Jokes" anymore: at least not around me, anyway. Those jokes were popular at the time. Of course, telling such jokes today will get you "Canceled" or maybe even fired. I never liked the kind of humor that required someone to be ridiculed. I get that it's part of growing up and it's supposed to thicken your skin for the challenges to your self-esteem that living in the world is going to present you with. But, for heaven's sake, doesn't the world present enough challenges on its own without having to manufacture even more?

Anyway, we discovered that a fellow student's first language was Polish, so I wrote a short speech and convinced him to come to the library and record it on our big old Wallensak tape recorder in his native language. I studied the tape for days and wrote it down phonetically so I could deliver it to the General Assembly in Polish. He was there when I did, and he was smiling. I hoped he was smiling because he enjoyed hearing his own language spoken by someone else and not because he had recorded a slew of foul language insults and thought it was funny. I got the feeling he was sincere, though. He wasn't laughing, he was just smiling proudly.

I was the first President of the Model UN General Assembly while I was at BoysTown. I helped Mr. Wehbey start it up because I was so into politics. I was also elected President of the Assembly for the Nebraska State Tournament one year. There were two schools that were voting for me. BoysTown's delegation voted for me, of course. The other was Central High School in Omaha. Their Debaters knew us well as we had beaten them as often as they had beaten us and there was some mutual respect there. What I was most proud of was that despite my many mistakes, I was always respected for how I ran assemblies. Being fair was a core value for me and I think the others could sense it. Everything I did in that position was filtered through that lens, and, of course, Roberts' Rules of Order.

At BoysTown, no one ever ran against me for the office, and I can only hope it was because they thought I was doing that good of a job. It's possible that no one else wanted the job because they wouldn't be able to debate, but I don't want to think about that right now.

The job was engaging and challenging. There was no time for lapses in concentration. You had to be on point the whole time. I liked that. It came naturally to me. It made me want to achieve excellence, which heretofore had been very much unlike me. I never liked competition until I got into debate and my motivation was more along the lines of not wanting to be embarrassed than to vanquish anybody. Of course, winning was cool, but it was never my driving force. It was more about self-preservation for me.

In High School I discovered that I really like sports that didn't involve competing. I wasn't good at any of them, but enjoyed doing them, nonetheless. I tried out for the swimming and the volleyball teams and didn't make the cut in either of them, but I kept doing them anyway, because I liked them. I liked Archery too, and ice skating, but swimming and diving were my favorites. I spent a great deal of time in the pool, having the time of my life, looking like a total idiot and not caring the least little bit about it. It all circled back to my love of all things graceful.

I barely passed physical education because I never developed upper body strength. I can say with confidence that I have never done a pull up in my entire life. Why I might be proud of that fact is for the psychoanalysts to mull over. That's too far above my pay grade. I was more interested in the boys who *could,* and the field house was chock full of them.

At BoysTown we all had to play intramural sports like baseball, basketball and football. Volleyball was one of them and it was the ONLY sport I enjoyed. I hated most of the sports we were required to play, in equal measure. I wasn't alone either. Most of us would slog through the required games as we competed against other cottages and sections. Unless Don Peer was on the baseball diamond. He loved the game so much that his enthusiasm would spread to most of the people on the field with him. The same was true of Julius Brinkley when it came to football.

We had our stars at BoysTown, just like any school does. The kids you look up to and strive to emulate; the kids who were exceptional and well regarded for something.

During my time at BoysTown it was Nate McKinney for Football and Don Peer for Baseball, of course. For Basketball, it was Tyrone Pryor, who had to be 7 feet tall and actually liked playing. He was a fierce competitor but was otherwise a sweet personality and the gentlest of souls. Nate McKinney was also a basketball star. He was an all-around sports guy and excelled at all of them. He was an athlete in the fullest sense of the word.

For Debate it was my Roommate Charles Larson. Larry Adams was a big shot in debate as well but he lived in another section.. I was in awe of Larson. He was my room mate in Cottage 22 and was a big part of the reason I stuck with debate. Everything about him was college bound. From about his belly button up to the top of his head was ravaged by acne. I used to hate it when he would beg me to pop the pimples that he couldn't reach. The fact that I would routinely do so was a testament to my admiration for him and to BoysTown's ethereal guidance for us to think of one another as brothers. They didn't really pound that message into us much; it was more like it was something that existed in the air around us. We were all boys, roughly the same age, with comparable histories that lived shoulder to shoulder in the same place. Debate was the one team in which I did make the cut. I did better and better as I progressed through High school too. It was my thing.

Debate was considered a sport at BoysTown. That always

seemed odd to me until my junior year when I was promoted to the Varsity squad and got my letter jacket with the big "B" for BoysTown on the front, and the concomitant street cred that goes with it. Suddenly, debate being a sport made all the sense in the world. I would go on to rank up to Larson's spot as he was graduating.

The interesting thing about stars in High School is that once they graduate, the door is automatically open to a whole new generation of stars to take their place from among the juniors who were then becoming seniors. It would happen to me in a few years too. A certain amount of reverence was expected towards the people who were ahead of you at BoysTown. It was kind of like the circle of life.

I was a gay kid who didn't know I was gay, or at least couldn't conceptualize that it could be OK to be gay because it wasn't. It was a sin, and if I didn't clean up my act, I would eventually go to hell for it. It's not like I could think outside the box and buck the system to be myself. The box was our whole lives. There wasn't anything outside of that. BoysTown made sure of it. First of all, I didn't know who I was, and it simply wasn't OK to be myself in the world in which I existed, even if I did.

Everybody else knew and would harass me about it every day. Of course, it was happening whether I liked it or not. I was a teenager and gay teenagers' hormones work just like everyone else's does. So, my high school years were filled with anxiety and self restraint.

I did have a boyfriend in high school though. I'll call him "Boyfriend" because he might still be with us, and I wouldn't want to complicate his life if he is. He and I ended up in a circle jerk one night in the basement of Cottage 22.

The room was lit by one candle. There were 5 of us and one boy, Diaz, had somehow talked us all in to a competition. He put a cookie on the floor and challenged us to jack off and the last person to cum on the cookie had to eat it. Boyfriend was with us and was all into the idea and cheered us on but wouldn't pull his dick out. I would learn later why, but everyone else did. I was the second one to let loose, but no one ended up eating the cookie. We gave the last guy a pass on having to eat it. I don't even remember who it was. It wasn't important.

While this was going on, Julius Brinkley was outside and happened to peek in the window well and saw us. I don't know what he was doing outside at that time of night, but he raced back into the cottage and casually sauntered downstairs to inquire as to what we were doing, acting as if he didn't already know.

After some hemming and hawing, we finally admitted what was happening. I was beside myself with excitement at the possibility that he might join us. We lobbied him to, and he didn't seem to be against the idea, but ultimately didn't. He was, after all, a good Catholic boy too, and an altar boy like me. I could understand why he wanted to but couldn't bring himself to do it. That was practically my life story. Besides, he was very conscious of his race. Maybe Brinkley thought it would be awkward to whip out his dick in front of us. He left us to our debauchery without seeming to make any judgment about it. He just smiled a little, wished us well, and went back upstairs.

We continued and after it was all over, we sat around for a while just talking and basking in the afterglow of an orgasm and the fact that we had gotten away with what amounts to a crime in Catholicism. I felt, for those few moments, like I really was one of the guys. That was rare for me. I usually felt like an outcast.

Later, Boyfriend would come to me and talk me into having some fun with him alone. We decided that Boyfriend would wake me up when everyone else went to sleep and we'd meet in the coatroom and have sex. Once there, we took our clothes off and he laid on top of me mission style, putting his dick between my legs and wiggled around until he came.

Boyfriend had a beautiful, sculpted body, he was a wrestler and worked out regularly, but he had a small dick. I suppose that was why he wouldn't pull it out with the rest of us at the circle jerk.

I wasn't having a problem with it because I was a teenager and I was having sex, voluntarily, no less! It was heaven for me. I'll never forget it. Of course, once the glow subsided, standard Catholic guilt would return, and I would vow to myself to never do it again. I regret how I had to struggle against a part of myself. Actually, having sex was wonderful while it was happening, but afterwards I'd always have this deep Catholic guilt that would have me hating myself for it.

After that, Boyfriend would wake me up and we would have fun many times, over our remaining years at BoysTown. So much for my vow! The only thing we did was jack each other off and we had to plan it ahead of time. We never did get caught so I guess you could say we pulled off our affair with panache. He offered to suck my dick one time, but I couldn't bring myself to cross that line. I was beating myself up enough already over mutual masturbation with him, so we just went on like that for the duration.

I hesitate to call him Boyfriend because that was all limited to the times when we were alone together. He was an alpha boy that was outwardly very macho. He was an Italian and I think that mattered to him. He mentioned it enough times. I wonder if he was struggling with what was happening inside him like I was. When others were around, he was condescending to me. Calling me the same homophobic slurs everyone else did. He posed a seamless front.

I don't know why I tolerated it. Didn't it ever occur to him that I could blow up his life, at any time, if I told on him? Of course, in order to do that I would have had to tell on myself too, and my life was socially precarious enough that I didn't really need to add that scandal to the list. I was upwardly mobile. We never did talk about that because I guess we had what you'd have to call a detente by mutually assured destruction. I really did love the times we spent alone, though. He was never selfish, he was always very considerate.

***

During my sophomore year Robert Kennedy was running for President and around Super Tuesday he visited BoysTown. I don't think I would call it a handshake, per se, but I did get to touch his hand in a swarm of fellow students that surrounded him during the entirety of his visit. I remember that there was a news story on TV around that time complaining that Robert Kennedy had to stop wearing cuff links and watches because people would steal them right off his body in swarms of people just like the one I was in that day. He was the political equivalent of a Rock Star. Everybody wanted to keep a piece of him. BoysTown held values much like the Kennedy Family's. They were Irish Catholics just like BoysTown's founder.

I have always admired the Kennedy Brothers, John, Robert and Ted. Here were three men who were born into wealth and exceptional privilege who, all three, dedicated their lives to leveling the playing field for people like me, who didn't have what they did. I realize that the Kennedy family wealth was built on illegal activity, and Yes, the Kennedy brothers each has their own moral failings. But I think that maybe Joseph Kennedy was trying to build a family that would become repentance for that fact. I still have respect and admiration for what these brothers accomplished to make the world a better place than they found it. The trajectory of my life when I was at BoysTown was to eventually go into politics and work toward the very same things that the Kennedy Brothers were doing. I felt a kinship with them, Robert in particular. He accurately saw the danger that the FBI posed to the country under J. Edgar Hoover. Hoover, at the time, had been conducting inappropriate and probably illegal surveillance of his older brother John, himself, Malcolm X, Reverend Martin Luther King, Students for a Democratic Society, The Merry Pranksters and just about anyone else who was involved with a protest against the War in Viet Nam.

***

Around this time, I was beginning to feel included in the core energy at BoysTown. I had developed a specialty that I loved, and my social circle began to widen. I wanted to make my new family proud. People knew who I was. It was like I was being included and even accepted despite my effeminacy. I was beginning to feel like an active, contributing member of my family.

CHAPTER 19

BoysTown Junior Year

Education was a big deal to the Catholic Church in the United States. As an orphan, I was, for all intents and purposes, raised by the Catholic Church. I was privileged to get an excellent education throughout my youth and the Catholic Church was responsible for all of it. I lived in 3 of the Catholic Schools I've attended and other placements along the way, were also Catholic, though not institutionally so, like BoysTown, St Francis Academy, Hall of the Divine Child and Our Lady Star of the Sea. These were Catholic Institutions.

For the bulk of my upbringing, I wore a uniform every day and dress blues on special occasions. In 1st grade I was taught how to tie a tie, shine shoes and otherwise behave with military decorum. It was part of my training and always expected of me. Although there were no uniforms at BoysTown we did have to wear ties to school. I was involved in competitive speech, so I would be wearing a tie and blazer quite often, anyway. I was now collegiate.

Authorities at BoysTown will swear that the institution is non-denominational, and I do not doubt that they believe that. But BoysTown is a very Catholic Institution. Or at least it was during the 4 years I lived there.

An example of what I mean is to compare the Dowd Chapel at BoysTown with the other space reserved for all other religions combined. One is a sizable free-standing cathedral, while the other is a room in the field house.

Anyone was welcomed and even encouraged to convert to Catholicism while at BoysTown, but I learned just how Catholic BoysTown was, when I went to Fr. Farrald and wanted to convert to the Bahai Faith. Fr. Farrald seemed to me to be the most approachable Priest about something like this. He was almost always a kind, thoughtful and supportive presence.

Although I was a varsity debater, with a letter jacket and everything, I anticipated some resistance to wanting to leave the Catholic Church. This wasn't just an experiment to see what would happen. I had become disillusioned with what the Church teaches, and I couldn't understand why we weren't allowed to read The Bible. We could only read Missals. Which always had the Catholic Church's interpretation of what the scriptures you just read, mean.

Some bible verses are never even mentioned and others, only parts. I can't tell you how many times I've heard a Priest, Nun or Brother quote me, *"Lean not unto your own understanding, in all your ways submit to him, and he will make your paths straight"* To me, it carried with it that "Him" refers to the Catholic Church or the Pope because all of the interpretations came from them. These were men, not Gods. If the Bible were the word of God, why would we need an interpreter?

I felt confident that I had all my ducklings in a row before I approached Fr. Farrald. I anticipated some gentle resistance to posing this idea and I was ready to defend myself. Poor Fr. Farrald, was not. He was caught off guard as he had very probably never had to answer that question before.

He began as calmly as I had always known him to be, but as we talked, he became more and more frustrated with me until he ended up yelling and pounding his fist on his desk. By this time in our conversation Fr. Farrald was having trouble restraining himself from jumping over his desk to choke me. The good Father finally invited me to leave his office and to take that foolishness with me. I did as directed, with my tail tucked between my legs.

***

I had my crushes like any other kid. Julius Brinkley of South Carolina and Michael Glover of Connecticut were the two that lived in my cottage. Both were black. Julius was a Dapper Dan. His skin was dark and always shiny. He moisturized daily and sported "Good Hair" that was always slick and meticulously in place. Today, you'd call him a "Metrosexual". He thought a great deal of himself and mostly with good reason. He had self-awareness enough to know what clothes made him look good. Suits!

He was a star football player and had the body of one. He was a delight to look at and he knew it. He also liked his ability to be social and entertaining. He could tell a good story and did so like it was second nature to him. His superpower was his charm. I so very much enjoyed being his friend. He knew I had a crush on him, but he never teased me about it and never played with my feelings. He liked me, and that was enough for me. He was one of my brothers.

I certainly did fantasize about Brinkley, though. He was the one who gave me the nickname "Professor". He was impressed with my debating skills and my command of English. He picked me to be his campaign manager when he ran for Mayor of BoysTown in our senior year. We won, too. Our platform was called "Acon and Beggs". We were fighting for having breakfast served at the Dining Hall on the weekends. Before that, we all had cereal at our leisure in the cottages. As it worked out, the kitchen staff agreed to serve breakfast on Saturday any time we felt like showing up, between 8 AM and noon. We could even order our eggs anyway we wanted, and the cooks would cook them to order, right there in front of us. Sunday, however, we were on our own because Sunday Mass took that time slot.

Glover was very different. He was a track and field guy. He was tall, thin, shapely and good natured. His resting pulse was casual and funny. You'd have to work hard to bump him off that center. He had a big dick, and he made sure everyone knew it. He would pull it out from time to time just to shock people. It wasn't a sexual thing; it was more to be playful and comically shocking. He obviously enjoyed the response.

In our room, he was often naked and seemed quite comfortable with it. I wasn't having any problem with that, either. I always had nice things to think about when masturbating. Glover's nickname was "Mona" after a character in the movie "Robinson Crusoe USN". Mona was the main character's pet monkey. Glover didn't seem to mind, and nobody was complaining that it was racist. That's the world we lived in at the time.

One kid who could take Glover from 0-60 in a matter of seconds was Alva Kline. Kline was our cottage commissioner in our Junior Year and there was no gray area about it. He was an alpha male. He was a big, thick lad with blond hair and blue eyes. He was hard on the surface, but there was a kindness just below it. I didn't like him because he was so domineering, and I imagine that's the problem Glover had with him as well. I think Kline really did love us and care about us in his way and could be tender and brotherly at infrequent times. He was kind of like an assistant manager to our house counselor. It was a student government position chosen by the counselor to help keep us in line. He had authority to tell us what to do, and more often, what not to do.

I remember a confrontation in our room one evening. Kline had come to the door of our room and was making some derogatory comment about Glover who was standing, fully naked, at his locker. They were yelling at one another because Glover wasn't fancying Kline's comment. I don't recall what Kline had said, but I'm reasonably sure it was racist.

Glover reached into his locker and produced a baseball bat and just stood there holding it at his side and glaring at Kline. Everything got really quiet. The tension was palpable. Kline had the good sense to take a beat, turned and walked away. That may be part of the reason why he was chosen commissioner of our cottage. He knew instinctively when it was time to back off. I don't think I ever gave him credit for how perceptive he was. He could read a room like it was second nature to him and instinctively know what to do; or in this case, what not to do.

Among the few regrets I will take to my grave has to be not taking Glover up on his offers, clumsy as they were, to have sex with him. He called me his "Little Heifer". He would flirt with me a lot over the two years we lived together in Cottage 22. It was always clandestine, of course. He was a year ahead of me and seemed to like me as much as I liked him.

At those times when it was just him and me, there was a connection between us that felt normal, brotherly, easy and warm. He knew I was lusting after him in a powerful way, but I was too repressed to allow what probably should have happened. He tried, but seemed to understand that I couldn't oblige because I was so Catholic. What was my problem? I was doing it with Boyfriend. Maybe it had to do with the fact that he was black and had a big dick and I wanted him too much. It was more fear than anything else.

The two times when I almost did do something with Glover we were blocked by the sudden appearance of Alva Kline! In the upstairs bathroom we used to take the curtain off one of the showers and drape it over the top of the other one, to make a kind of sauna. One night Glover and I were in the sauna. He was on a chair in the shower with his big dick and beautiful body and I asked to join him. I sat on the floor of the shower next to him and, just between you and me, I had *plans*.

It wasn't long before Kline burst into the bathroom and quickly flung open the curtain. He was certain that he had caught us in a compromising situation. Fortunately, neither of us were hard yet and Kline just asked what we were doing. Glover snapped some comment back at him that must have been enough for Kline because he turned and walked out. The timing was perfect because I was just about to make a move when Kline burst in. After Kline interrupted us, we were too scared to try it for fear that Kline would be nearby ready to pounce.

The other time we almost had sex was when Boyfriend, who I was already having somewhat of an affair with, asked me who in the cottage I wanted to jack off. I told him Glover, of course. Boyfriend immediately went and told Glover who was in a different room than me at the time. The cottage counselors would move us around from time to time. Glover was excited at the prospect. He came to me immediately and we decided, under the excited gaze of Boyfriend, to meet in the upstairs bathroom after everyone was asleep.

The time came when I was sure the coast was clear. I walked into the bathroom and there stood Boyfriend and Glover with his big dick, graceful body and beautiful smile. Oh my God, this was finally going to happen. My prayers were about to be answered. Just as we started discussing what we were going to do, in walks Alva Kline! It wasn't rocket science to figure out why Glover and I disliked him.

Kline immediately demanded to know what we were doing. Glover glared at him and snapped something to the effect of, "We're in the bathroom, stupid, we got up to go pee! We don't need you to supervise us." He was convincing enough that Kline just looked at us suspiciously for a beat and then demanded that we disband and get to bed. He followed us out of the bathroom and waited at his bedroom door until we were settled in.

Glover and I never did get to play with one another. He graduated shortly thereafter. I was crushed. I had finally allowed myself to indulge in what would have been a truly wonderful experience and one that I had frequent dreams about for 2 years and Kline had blocked us *again*!

I think it would have been a good experience because there was nothing menacing about Glover. I don't think he was gay. I had seen him around girls at the Junior and Senior Proms. He clearly liked them too. He just liked sex, I guess, and the gender of the object of his interest didn't appear to matter much. This was all good-natured fun to him and I suspect it would have been fun for me too. But, I'm sure I would have beaten myself up about it afterwords like I was doing with Boyfriend.

Glover didn't have the same brutal conflict I had about indulging that part of himself. He seemed free of any of the stuff I was having such an intense struggle with. That struggle would continue until I was 28.

I sometimes wonder what Boyfriend's interest in all of this was. He was setting me up to have sex with someone besides him. That didn't make sense to me. If he wouldn't pull his little weenie out in front of us during the circle jerk, I doubt seriously that he would be willing to pull it out in front of Glover. Glover had the biggest dick in the whole house, and everybody knew it. Did he just want to watch us, like he did in the basement last year? I don't know, and I doubt that it matters in the scheme of things.

CHAPTER 20

BoysTown Senior Year

The only kids I knew that may have had a more rigid education than us were the Jewish Kids at Central High. I debated many of them throughout my high school years and they were no joke. In fact, if it wasn't for Kirschenbaum and Lear, Brian McGinty and I would have taken state, our senior year. The State Tournament came down to them & us and it ended up being them.

The four of us, Kirschenbaum, Lear, Brian and I, had a mostly collegian relationship with one another, despite our competition. They recognized us as a team not to be taken lightly, and we felt the same about them, having met them many times in battle.

McGuinty and I were able to handle most other teams we were up against with relative ease. Our two-pronged approach was our super-power. McGuinty was the brains on our team and he knew he wasn't that good at oration. I provided the dramatic ethos. Most of my life at BoysTown was tied to public speaking and I had gotten pretty good at it over the years. To most other schools we competed against, debate wasn't their priority, and it wasn't a sport that you could get a letter jacket for. For them, it was more of a supplement to whatever else they were gearing up for in their education. To us, it was what we lived and breathed.

There was mutual respect between the four of us. We would often chide one another with comments we hoped would be witty. Like the time Brian and I happened to pass them in the hallway at a tournament. They were sitting on the stairs intently working out a strategy for their next debate. I nudged Brian as we walked by and said, in a voice I hoped would be loud enough for them to hear, "Brian, look at Kirschenbaum and Lear over there diligently falsifying evidence for their next debate!" "Hard workers, those two." Without skipping a beat, Kirschenbaum shot back, "We never have to work this hard when we debate YOU guys!" "These guys might even give us a challenge!"

Kirschenbaum & Lear were our arch-enemies all 4 years. Sometimes we won, and sometimes they did, as we were evenly matched and all 4 of us were Varsity Debaters. The pendulum had obviously swung in their direction as our Senior year came to a close.

During the State Championship debate, The fellows were throwing points and quotes at us rapid fire, like a machine gun; *lots* of them! We were all excited knowing we could refute all of their arguments without breaking a sweat. Brian, soldier that he was, stood up and fired back, point for point. He just kept going all the way until the buzzer went off. I was so proud of him.

We were so sure we had just taken state, against Central High, no less! We were the best debaters in the state. We were proving that these orphan boys from BoysTown have some game! It was a thrilling and exciting moment! Accent on "Moment". We hadn't seen our score cards yet.

Kirschenbaum & Lear didn't do a better job than usual, but we, or more specifically Brian, was so busy refuting everything Kirschenbaum & Lear had just said that he forgot to give our plan. Our scorecard indicated that we were awfully good that day. One judge even wrote that we should have won, but not giving a plan was our fatal mistake. As it turns out, our arch enemies could have sucked rocks in that debate and still took state.

Of course, they *could* have, but they didn't. They were the sharp and formidable opponents they had always been, and the pendulum had simply swung in their direction, this time. It was their turn to crow on us, and they did, just like we were planning to them, just a few minutes ago.

Brian and I sadly accepted our 2nd place trophy and shuffled off back to BoysTown with our tails tucked between our legs. Principle Mitt Stoefel proudly placed our 2nd place trophy in the big glass case in the High School Lobby. Our teachers and classmates were quite a bit more excited about it than Brian and I were. We knew how close we had come to pillaging the entire state of Nebraska.

There's an old saying on one of those inspirational posters you find at work. "When you're up to your ass in alligators, it's difficult to remember that your initial objective was to drain the swamp!" That played into my life quite comfortably at that moment. I was on the second-best debate team in the whole state of Nebraska, for crying out loud! Why in the world was I moping about it?

I had been so busy with my head in the books for the last 4 years that I hadn't noticed that I had gradually become good at debate! I mean, *really* good! Better than my mentor, Charles Larson! As good as he was, he didn't rank in the State Tournament when his time came up. I was actually good at something and hadn't really thought about it until just then!

I was also awakening to the fact that I was a social being. I wanted to be one of the guys but was hampered by being in a struggle against my true nature. I was gay in a world where there was no such thing. Or at least there was no such thing that could be explored. No one I knew was gay.

Of course, there were other gay students at BoysTown, but no one identified themselves as such. If anyone knew they were gay, they were hiding it out of a sense of survival just like I was. There were no role models to emulate, or anyone I could talk to about it. When I tried, the response was always the same. There was something morally wrong with me and my only option, as a good Catholic boy, was to "Pray away the Gay". I stopped trying to talk about it altogether. It became clear that I was on my own about the subject of sexuality.

I had dates with girls. It was practically required. My Sophomore year I was with a girl named Priscilla Hect. A big girl who was clearly in charge of all she could see. That's how we ended up together. She picked me and I didn't fight back. I was called upon to date a girl and I guess she was as good as any to a guy who wasn't interested to begin with.

My school mates didn't like her much because she was big and I was teased relentlessly about taking her to a dance. Dating girls was always so uncomfortable for me because there was nothing about it that was even tangentially connected to the life I was living. I was doing it because I was expected to. It was a charge that I had to do.

The thing I hated most about social gatherings at BoysTown is that they always seemed so contrived. We would either be bused to a girl's school, or they would be bused to our school. It seemed sad and desperate to me because your only options were the girls who were there at that moment. There was precious little opportunity to meet someone at random with whom there might be actual chemistry.

My senior year it was Janelle Evans. I did like her! She was a budding poet and seemed to like how much I wanted to be President of The United States. She was short, shapely, open and pretty but she was somewhat of an outcast in her school too, because she was very much an artist type. She was a little weird and completely comfortable with it. She had a very strong constitution. I can only guess that she had good parents who loved her just like she was. She was lucky like that!

As I was graduating, she wrote me a poem about how our Prom was, for her. Aside from her "fall" falling off while we were dancing, it was nearly perfect.

Janelle's poem was the stuff of romantic fantasies. Disney could have written it for her. Of course, I was just following along. That fantasy was all her and it was near perfect. I do hope she eventually found a man that was worthy of her. I wish I could have been sorry that it wasn't going to be me.

My involvement with girls was mainly debate. I debated lots of girls. Few sent me home empty handed but, gratefully, none seemed interested in me as a boy, either. My interactions with them were mostly cool because of it. Girls make great friends unless they have designs on me. Then it becomes uncomfortable. But I really did enjoy Janelle's company. With her, there was also the added bonus, back at home, that she was pretty enough that the other boys didn't tease me like they did when I was with Priscilla.

Of all people, "Boyfriend" was our Cottage Commissioner my senior year and the reason I ran away from BoysTown the only time I did. We didn't have a Cottage Counselor for a while and Boyfriend was the only authority in the cottage. He had turned loose the dogs of war and no one, including me, was safe. For days, violent and otherwise abusive incidents were gradually erupting in Cottage 22 under Boyfriend's watchful eye. It was clear who the toxic alpha males among us were. Boyfriend let them out of their cages. The rest of us were in a state of constant anxiety waiting for them to dial us into their cross-hairs.

Several of the more aggressive boys caught me in the basement one evening, threw a blanket over me so I couldn't see that was happening and they all started beating me. Punches and kicks were coming from all directions, seemingly all at once. It was probably only a few seconds but felt like hours. It was a horrendous experience being blinded, beaten and helpless. They didn't break any bones, but I had plenty of visible injuries and everything hurt. But the horror of it all and the probability that it would happen again was more than I was willing to abide.

I couldn't report them because I couldn't see who was doing it. Besides, who would I report it to, Boyfriend? I had been through this before, with the Schmidt's, and I wasn't about to allow it to happen again. I had grown enough, by that time, to realize that I could refuse to accept it. This time, unlike with the Schmidts, there was no threat of death hanging over my head like a Sword of Damocles.

As much as I loved being at BoysTown, this was more than I was willing to go through again. If I'm not safe in my own home, where could I go to find safety? Me and another boy took off and went to the only place in Omaha that I knew of, Debra Whitaker's house.

I had gone to a dance with her once and we hit it off really well. I would see her from time to time when we were released onto the streets of Omaha on a day pass. I learned a few years later that she was a lesbian. That probably played into why we hit it off so well as friends.

***

BoysTown would pile a bunch of us onto a bus and turn us loose in Omaha, if our behavior was good enough, with the caution that we were to be back on that bus, ready to go home by no later than 5PM.

At 5PM that bus would pull out and if you weren't on it, you were AWOL. This would occasionally work out to be a problem for anyone who had used their $5 to buy alcohol and got drunk. At BoysTown, we had our "Stoners" just like any other school did. Sometimes one or two would show up at the bus under the influence of something and would be in relatively serious trouble.

I know what you're thinking and, NO, that never happened to me. It did happen to Danny Presnell once, in our senior year, though. We were downtown and it was about 10AM. Danny was coming hard at me to go with him to buy some Mescal. I wouldn't do it. I must have been a Good Catholic Boy that day and that pissed him off, so we split up for the day. It turned out that he did find somebody to buy it for him and he showed up at the bus, smelling of alcohol and breath mints. Not a good day for Danny, but I felt vindicated in my resistance to his lobbying earlier that day. That, and there are few joys more delicious to me than being able to say, "I told you so!"

***

Anyway, back to my story. My run-a-way partner and I woke Debbie and her parents up in the middle of the night and they sat us all down at the dining room table to talk it out. They made us some coffee and toast and listened to me as I described what had happened and told them the story of the kid who had suffered a blanket party at Camp Okajobi last summer and ended up with injuries serious enough that he had to be removed from BoysTown altogether.

The Whitakers were horrified at my story and set us up on couches in the basement for the night. The next morning they fed us breakfast and took us back to BoysTown. They wouldn't release us to the social workers until they were assured that the violence would stop. We had a new Counselor in Cottage 22 later that same day and Boyfriend was fired from being our cottage commissioner.

Today, this type of thing would get you thrown in jail. But this was 1970 and the prevailing attitude, even at BoysTown, was still "Boys will be Boys". It really wasn't that big of a deal. The police were not called, and it was all handled quietly.

***

Overall, I enjoyed my senior year, mainly because of the collegiate pecking order of how BoysTown society worked. It was mostly easier on me than it had been in earlier years. I didn't get harassed nearly as much and was treated with at least a modicum of respect. I was a senior. I was among the elite now. For Example, on our debate squad, I was looked up to by underclassmen just like I had looked up to Charles Larson and Larry Adams when I was coming up. It was tradition.

This would be the first time in my life when I would be able to see the transition. Before this, I would end one grade and enter a different school for the next. Sometimes I would be transferred in the middle of the school year and have to try to catch up to the rest of the class. There was no time to try and find a mentor or someone to look up to. I was in survival mode for the lion's share of my youth.

For four years at BoysTown, I got to watch as upperclassmen graduated and be replaced by juniors becoming seniors. Now, it was my turn. That felt good. It felt like the way things *should* be. It was the circle of life and I had never experienced that before I came to BoysTown.

Graduation day had finally arrived. There were just over 100 of us standing in the High School hallway in our Robes and Mortars waiting to be escorted into the Auditorium. The emotional environment of that wait had me at the very brink of tears the whole time we waited.

Here were my brothers, these guys that I've been through so much with over the past 4 years. We lived together in ways that most people don't. We ate together, went to school together, went to Mass together, we were on sports teams together, we went to Prom together, we even went to summer camp together. I loved some of them and equally hated others, Just like in any normal family. But at the end of the day, these were my brothers, and it was beginning to hit me. I'm probably never going to see *any* of them again. I knew the feeling well, it had happened to me, years before, and it doesn't feel good. In fact, it hurts in a deeply personal place.

While I'm standing there struggling not to cry, here comes Kim Lump. An Asian boy who was always there, but never really noticed. I think you know the type. He's stealthy. He had accomplished a lot over the last 4 years. He was involved with just about everything going on at BoysTown, but he did it quietly. Maybe it was a cultural thing for him. He didn't seem to think that he had anything to do with his accomplishments. It was more than just humility.

The poor kid was crying. Not regular crying, mind you. I'm talking about "Viola Davis", "Hot Mess", "Bubble Snot, Ugly Crying". He was going up to a bunch of us, each at random, to tell us how much we meant to him and how much he was going to miss us. He went on and on about how we were never going to see one another again after we are escorted into that Auditorium. He was saying what many of us were feeling but wouldn't dare say out loud, on a bet. We needed Lump to do that.

Try as I might to buck up under the pressure, I quietly released the tears to roll down my face at will. A good handful of my brothers let loose as well. Lump was right. This may be it, for all of us.

This was the first school that I had ever attended for more than a full school year. When I got here, I was a thoroughly messed up gay kid, a candidate for the loony bin and didn't have the remotest idea who I was. Today I'm standing, shoulder to shoulder, with my brothers as an equal. I was known for things. I was a Library Assistant, a Champion Debater and Model UN President of the Assembly. I had an identity! I was "The Professor"! Standing in that Hallway were just over 100 other boys with similar stories of love and hate, anger and peace, fear and courage, all of us having the same experience and living it in a hundred different ways. But every last one of us were having this experience together. That is what BoysTown had done for us.

The moment had arrived, and we were ceremoniously escorted into the auditorium. At the time, when you graduated from BoysTown, your graduation gifts from the home were $250 and a one way ticket to anywhere in the continental United States that we wanted to go. We weren't required to go back to where we came from if we didn't want to. It was a striking reminder that once we left that auditorium, we were, in every imaginable way, On Our Own!

The mixed feelings were intense. On one hand, I was overjoyed to be set free, and on the other, I was terrified that I was on my own for the first time in my life and what would happen to me next was entirely up to me! Not some Catholic social workers having a private conversation in another room. I had built a little bit of confidence in myself at BoysTown, but certainly not enough for *that*!

I don't remember the ceremony at all. But I did walk away with a beautiful gold class ring that I accidentally left in a bowling alley restroom a year later, while washing my hands. I also had a very nice leather-bound High School Diploma from a reputable school and a bus ticket back to Detroit.

Later that evening, Danny Presnell and I were in a motel room waiting for morning when we were to board transportation to where we would begin our new, independent lives. He and I were brothers like that. There were several of our graduating brothers staying at the same motel and for the same reason. Danny was lobbying me hard to switch out my bus ticket and move to Arizona with him. I resisted despite his persistence. I was certain that my family would take me back and everything would finally be OK. When I had finally convinced him that I was going home to Detroit, he gave up and went out to buy some alcohol.

While he was gone, in walked Boyfriend who started in on

me with the same lobbying Danny had done. Only Boyfriend wanted me to move to Alabama with him. There was a little more to *his* lobbying because he and I had been having sex for the last two years. He was, essentially, my boyfriend. I wasn't having that either. I had other plans. I was, at long last, going home.

Boyfriend wanted to get busy right there, one last time, but I wasn't into it because I was certain that Danny would come walking in right as we would have been standing there with our dicks out, looking like a couple of deer caught in the headlights. Besides, I wasn't in a conducive head space to think about sex right then. I was far too emotional.

The next morning, all three of us got up and tearfully went our separate ways; Boyfriend to Alabama, Danny to Arizona and me to Detroit.

CHAPTER 21

Coming Home

I had just arrived at the Greyhound Bus Terminal in Detroit, and I was on top of the world! I felt excited and ready! I had a few phone numbers of people in what used to be my family and I needed a place to stay so I started making calls from a phone booth just outside the terminal. I called Mom first then Grandma Hutch and neither of them answered. My dad didn't answer either. Cell phones and/or answering machines were still somewhere off in the future. This was June of 1970. I began to feel the earth crumbling a little beneath my feet. The exhilaration I had felt just moments ago was dissipating by the minute as I went through the few phone numbers I had.

Of all the Schroeders, it was Aunt Jo who had kept the most consistent tabs on me throughout my childhood. She could tell you where I was at any time in this journey except for my location when I was in a standard Foster Family like the Schmidts or the Macklems. She knew I was in a Foster placement, but likely didn't know specifically where those families were.

I called her, certain that she would be the one who would come and get me. She answered the phone and the ensuing conversation was the most soul crushing conversation I have ever had, before or since. It would be a defining moment in my life. Things would never be the same after that conversation. It happened that the change ended up being a very good one, but I had no way of knowing that at the time. Aunt Jo certainly did though. She's gone now, but I can't thank her enough for what she did for me that day.

There was, of course, the small talk, but when I finally told her where I was and that she could come and get me now, she carefully declined. It's funny when I think about now, how I just automatically assumed that someone in the Schroeder family would drop everything and welcome me home with open arms after all the opportunities they had to do so while I was growing up. It wouldn't be until later that it would occur to me that the Schroeders never really were my family. I was a kid that they had taken in for a season, much like the other foster families. I wasn't actually related to any of them.

"I know you, Greg." She said, "If I come and get you now, you will never learn to stand on your own two feet." "I know things have been bad for you for a long time and my heart goes out to you right now." "What happened to you isn't fair and nobody should have to go through what you've been through." she continued, "But if you don't do this now, you never will and you deserve to have a better life than that." She assured me that I had the strength and the intelligence, and it was time to put all of that to good use.

As we hung up the phone I began to cry, right there in that phone booth on Woodward Avenue. I was petrified! I couldn't move. "What would become of me?" I thought. Oh my God, here I am *again,* left alone with no one that I knew yesterday! This time, there's no Mr. Fox, no family to go home to, no one waiting to receive me, nowhere to live. I'm not even in a familiar neighborhood and I didn't know how to get to a neighborhood that I *was* familiar with. Besides, what could I possibly do if I did find somewhere familiar from so long ago? There would be no one there who knew me.

I wasn't thinking about the fact that throughout my entire life I had depended on someone else to take care of me, albeit in horrible circumstances at times, but none the less, there had always been someone that was accountable for me. I had never had to rely on myself for *anything*. Everything had always been handed to me. Even my clothes, for Christ's sake!

I sat there crying in that phone booth for what must have been hours. Eventually, I began to tire and gradually realized that I had some choices to make. I couldn't just sit there crying for the rest of my life. I could just see the headlines; "Detroit native graduates from High School and dies, crying, in phone booth on Woodward Ave."

I had to come out of that phone booth and *do something*! I was 18 years old, I was able-bodied and the diploma right there in my suitcase suggested that I was, at least, relatively intelligent. There was no legitimate reason for me to think that this would be as far as I would go in life. I slowly began to actualize that I was on my own now, in the only way that mattered.

Slowly, at first, I began to pull myself together and make some decisions about what I was going to do right now, today, to proceed with my life. I needed a place to lay my head and something to eat. I wiped the tears from my face as best I could and at the suggestion of a fellow traveler at the bus terminal, I got a room at the YMCA, a few blocks away. It cost only a few dollars a night and I still had most of the $250 that I got from BoysTown for graduation. That $250 was a decent sized chunk of money in 1970.

When I got up the next morning, everything felt a little bit more possible than it had the day before. I had a vague concept of what to do next. I needed a job and a place to live. I got a phone book and found a motel room at the corner of 8 Mile and Telegraph Road, right next to a "Bob's Big Boy" because it was cheap enough to hold me over until I could find some work. I called a cab and off I went.

I had never looked for work before. Although I had done a *lot* of work in my life, every bit of it had been handed to me. I never once had to look for it. I decided that I would start at that corner by the Bob's Big Boy and walk down 8 Mile Road and stop at every business on both sides of the street and ask for work. I did that every day for several hours and then return to the motel when I got tired. I don't recall how many days I was out there, but I got all the way to Mound Road before someone said, "Yes!"

I walked into Mound Lanes, and sheepishly asked for a job. My job up to that point was being told "No" for several hours every day since I got back to Detroit. I wasn't the least bit ready for what happened next.

A youngish man with curly brown hair and the unkempt appearance of a mechanic, looked up from painting a ball return cover. He stood up and handed me a paint roller and a bucket of white paint and pointed at a wall separating the lanes from the attached bar and simply said, "Paint that wall." He didn't even ask my name. I said, "Thank you!" and went about painting the wall as he had directed.

My Mechanic friend ended up being the bowling alley pinsetter mechanic/manager. His name was Steve and when we had finished for the day, he went to the bowling alley cash register, handed me $10 and told me to return tomorrow. Over the next week or so, he taught me how to rebuild AMF Pinsetters. When we finished one, we'd move on to the next and he would explain what we were doing and why, each step of the way. There were 22 in all, and thankfully, not all of them needed to be rebuilt. I was enjoying the work and the education. Steve and I were feeling a sense of accomplishment with the testing of each machine as we finished rebuilding it. We'd go out front and bowl a few lines to make sure the machine was functioning properly, and then enjoy a celebratory Pabst Blue Ribbon and then move on to the next one. I was in an environment that reminded me of a brief time in my life, long ago, when I was feeling some joy.

CHAPTER 21

After trying me out with the painting and the pinsetters, Steve offered me a position at $50 a week. New owners had just taken over operation of the business and he needed staff to run the place. I grew up in a bowling alley, as you might recall, so I felt right at home and after all the painting and pinsetter mechanizing was done, I was made the daytime counterman. I worked there, 6 days a week, for the next year.

After work I would scour the want ads looking for a place nearby. I finally found a two-bedroom place about 3 blocks from Mound Lanes and met Borgia, the landlord. He was a Jewish immigrant from one of the Soviet bloc countries and spoke with a heavy accent. He called me something that sounded like Greyhory. He played the Cello and made his own wine in his basement. There was no contract or background check involved. Everything was done with a handshake. I don't think he even knew my last name.

My rent receipt every month would be a bottle of red wine and some good conversation. Borgia had lots of interesting stories about his life back home. He kept a key to the house and would frequently stop by to check on his rental. It didn't take me long to figure out that his frequent inspections had nothing to do with security. He was a lonely old man that just wanted to have someone to talk to. He was an interesting and loving fellow, so I wasn't having a problem with it. I had nothing that I felt a need to hide from him anyway and I didn't have any friends yet either. The arrangement worked out fine for both of us.

The apartment was sparse. There was a bed and a dresser in the bedroom and an old bench from a bus in the living room. There was a card table and two folding chairs in the dining room. That was the extend of the furniture.

After a few months of clumsily running my own life, I became somewhat comfortable with the idea. I called Aunt Jo and told her about it. She was excited and wanted to know everything.

She came to see my apartment and the place where I worked. I had to admit that it was good to see her and to realize that she was the same Aunt Jo she had always been.

She made suggestions and offered some furniture for my barren living space. The cabin up north had been sold, years before when Grandma Schroeder passed away and all of the furniture was in storage at Clinton Gables. We loaded up a couch and chair and the famous coffee table. The table wasn't young and fresh anymore, though. It had weathered much like I had. When I lived at the cabin, it was new and had a piece of glass that covered the surface, which was now gone. A hole had been drilled down through the center of it to accommodate a pole lamp. The sight of it made me feel warm inside. It had a kind of primal familiarity to me.

Aunt Jo also found me a TV set in storage from one of the rooms of the hotel, which was now closed due to a fire a few years earlier. A lot had changed since I had been removed from the family. The TV was the most wonderful piece of furniture. Dark polished wood with speaker baffles encased in the bottom that made it look like a studio set for a TV Variety show. The picture tube was the largest that they made at the time; probably 19 inches. The sound was deep, smooth and luxurious.

We hauled all of that back to Warren and spent the better part of the day setting up house for me. A few weeks later she invited me to her and Uncle Bill's new house in Mt. Clemens. The family had grown from Kathy, Billy and Danny, to include Jaymie, Robby and the twins. It was a big new house and it even had built in intercoms. The living room was beautiful, almost like a fairy tale. We weren't even allowed to walk through it. There were plastic covers on all the white Louis the XIV furniture and it was only used for special occasions.

Aunt Jo had also invited my brother Mike. I suspect that she had secretly arranged it to see what would happen, she knew that we hadn't seen each other since we were young children. Things were a little weird between me and Mike. We hadn't seen each other face to face since the divorce.

When we found ourselves together at Aunt Jo's that day, I was 18 and he had just turned 20. We had both grown up completely apart. Inside, we knew that we should love one another because we are brothers and had been through a lot together in a very short amount of time in our formative years, yet we also felt like strangers because, in fact, we were.

We spent the day sort of communicating through our younger cousins and Aunt Jo, hardly ever addressing one another directly. It just felt too strange. Both of us wanting so badly to say what neither of us knew how to verbalize, but both felt so deeply you could cut the atmosphere with a knife. It was during this visit that I learned that the two Schroeder families couldn't stand one another. They were unquestionably in opposing camps. The Uncle Bill Schroeders had never forgiven the Les & Betty Schroeders for what they had done to me and Mike and me and Mike were a couple of extra pieces that didn't really fit in either camp. When I said that our family had scattered to the winds, I had no idea how *much* that was true.

Later that day, Mike and a friend of his were giving me a ride home to Warren. He pulled a joint out of his pocket and suggested that I smoke it with him and his friend. I was so terrified that I demanded that he stop the car and let me out.

This took him completely by surprise. He promised to put the joint away and begged me to stop freaking out. But I would not be consoled, I was a good little Catholic boy and good little Catholic boys do not smoke pot, or even hang around with people who do. I was terrified! Against his pleading, I got out of the car and hitch-hiked back to Warren. That was the last time I saw my brother Mike until over 30 years later.

***

Mound lanes had its share of Characters as well. The new owner was a fellow named Paul Mobley. He was a tall friendly middle-aged man that took a liking to me after learning that I was an orphan and had come up through the Foster System. His story was very similar. He took me under his wing and over the year that I worked there, I gradually began to realize that he was a mob boss.

Another of his employees was a Former prize-fighter named Tiger Jones. Tiger was a sweetheart of a man around me. He was a friendly good looking and muscled-up black man that seemed to have a new and beautiful woman on his arm every week or so. He was Paul's bodyguard, so he was around a lot and seemed to take a liking to me, too.

He had warm and protective vibes and a charismatic personality. He smiled a lot and loved to laugh. I'm glad I never got to see him man-handle anyone, although it was obvious that he could when he needed to. He took me to his house one afternoon when he was in a hurry to dress up to prepare for some event later that night. It was in a scary part of town, but the vibe of the place was just like him. It was pleasant, warm, clean and just a little bit pretentious. I guess you'd call it showy.

Back at Mound Lanes, Paul had set up office in what was once, the Pro Shop and I ended up being his receptionist by default. He taught me some techniques on how to politely put off a caller that he didn't want to talk to. Those skills would come in handy later in my life, too. I've had many jobs where I needed to know how to do that.

Our janitor/handy man was an old drunk guy named Stanley. He was tall, thin and wiry with a disheveled, dirty look about him. He looked homeless and he kind of was. He was always around. It didn't take long to notice that he was not an educated man. Some of it may have been the result of a lifetime of overindulgence with beer and wine.

Mound Lanes had apparently inherited Stanley from the previous owners. When he was needed for something, we would just go out to his house and get him. He lived in the back parking lot in a little shed that the previous owners had built for him. Tiny Houses are nothing new. I would even live in one for a short spell years later.

Stanley worked for a small daily allowance and free beer and meals. I would be the one to pay him from the cash register at the end of my workday. I think it was something like $5 a day. I'm pretty sure that free beer was the main draw that kept him there. He was a friendly sort, and although he was old, he could be pretty scrappy if anyone got unruly in the bowling alley.

I saw him "Invite" a drunken bowler to leave, one afternoon, who had been getting a bit too friendly with one of the bartender/waitresses. He certainly made short work of it. The bar staff were all young beautiful women and their uniforms, if you could call them such, were emaciated bikinis. There would be four or five of them needed to cover the lunch hour, because,,,

Mound Lanes sat between 2 Chrysler manufacturing plants and lunch time was a madhouse. The guys would come over on lunch break, have a sandwich, maybe play some pool, drink a bunch of beer, smoke some pot out back in the parking lot and then go back to work. Seeing their condition when they left Mound Lanes, I decided right then and there, that I would never by a Chrysler! EVER!

At home, I was enjoying my life pretty well. I had gotten a Longines Symphonette stereo from one of those record clubs, where they send you a record every month and then bill you for it. Most of what they sent me were good choices, but sometimes I'd get something I wasn't interested in, and I'd often get behind in my payments. I wasn't yet very good at managing money, but I got it right enough that I have never been evicted. I loved music and that little stereo was my dealer; my best friend, even more than that beautiful TV that Aunt Jo had given me.

After about a year of working for Paul Mobley at the bowling alley, it was beginning to dawn on me that I was too close to criminal and/or violent activities. I was getting a bit nervous about it, too. Paul, to his credit, had always been careful to keep his other business concerns at arm's length from me. I was an insider to this group and a favorite of the boss, so I was kept safe from harm. But not all of Paul's associates were as discrete. I had begun overhearing some conversations that caused me some alarm.

Just then, I got a call from Danny Presnell, whom, as you might recall, had gone back home to Phoenix after we graduated from BoysTown. He was *still* lobbying me to move to Phoenix and the life he was describing sounded like a lot of fun. I knew I didn't want to stay where I was. I was having terrifying visions of people, maybe even me, being fitted with cement shoes and tossed into the Detroit River in the dead of night. I had actually overheard one of Paul's associates say that very thing, recently. I wanted no part of it!

I went to Paul and begged him to let me go. In my young and inexperienced mind, I thought that if you try to leave the mob and you know things, they would have to kill you to keep you from snitching. All I knew about the mob, at that point, had been gathered from gangster movies and TV shows.

I was terrified and wanted out. I guess Paul was unaware that some of his associates had been having somewhat loose lips around me. He was shocked that I was in such distress and clearly didn't understand why. He had always been careful to keep me out of it. I told him about the call from Danny and that I wanted to move to Arizona. He got up, walked over to me and gave me a nice hug. He told me that he was sorry to see me go and had me wait while he wrote me a check for $200 and wished me well. "As long as I'm around, nothing bad will ever happen to you" he promised. "If you ever need anything, you have my number."

Aside from the previous few weeks when I began to hear things that frightened me, I was happy for the whole year I worked at Mound Lanes. I had the confidence of knowing that I *could* take care of myself, and I *could* make my own way in the world.

I had made *one* commitment to myself as I was graduating from BoysTown a year ago, and it was that I would never live with violence again. I've kept that commitment ever since. I still remember making that promise, too. It was a lot like that scene in the middle of "Gone with the Wind" just before the intermission, where Scarlett O'Harra, standing under that tree with her clenched fist, defiantly straining toward the sky, swearing, "As God as my witness, I will never go hungry again!"

Along the way, there have been times, things, and occasionally people, that I've had to give up to keep that promise. But having long since made it, I regret nothing I've ever had to do to keep it. The next morning, I packed my bags and boarded a plane to Sky Harbor Airport.

In Phoenix, Danny already had a place with a few friends who needed one more roommate to share the rent. Life in Phoenix turned out to be everything Danny had promised it would be. I had a truly wonderful time living there, and I'll tell you all about that one day. Of course, there have been ups and downs along the way but suffice it to say, for now, that my life gradually kept getting better from there.

Years later, I finally settled the war going on inside me between being Catholic and being gay. I still yearned to be worthy in the eyes of God as best I knew, but try as I always had, I simply could not stop what was happening inside me. I was twenty-eight years old and I was sitting in a lounge chair in a house in Arizona. My feet were propped up on the living room windowsill and I took a puff of my cigarette.

***

There's an old story about a Native warrior speaking with his young son. His son seemed troubled and as they walked along together, the warrior looked down at his son, and calmly spoke as if to another adult, "There is a war being waged between two wolves in the heart of every man." he said. "One is a good wolf, and the other is a bad one." There was a pause as the boy considered what his father had just said. After a moment the son looked up at his father and asked, "Who wins the war?" The boy's father took another step, stopped, and looked lovingly into his son's eyes. "The one you feed." He quietly said.

There had been a war going on inside me for my entire life between what I had always been and what I had always been taught to be! Sitting there kicked back in that chair, I realized right down to the tips of my toes that I simply could not go on like this. The war itself was killing me. I was reminded of the last time this had happened to me. It was ten years ago in that phone booth outside the bus terminal in Detroit. I knew I had to make a decision and the time had finally come that it had to be *now*! My life depended on it.

I considered that accepting my myself would separate me from the love of God. Or so I had always been taught by the very people who had raised me; the people I looked up to for guidance, and direction and, yes, even for love. Even society was aligned with them. They *all* agreed that if I surrendered to my true nature, I was doomed to a tragic life of self-destruction followed by an eternity of burning in a lake of fire!

For the first time in my life, I considered the possibility that The Holy Catholic Church might have been mistaken. What if they were just reflecting what *they* had always been taught and wanted the best for me? What if they were only trying to guide me along the only path *they* knew? What if their intentions were pure and they simply didn't know any better? Was it even possible that I *could* know something that they didn't? That was a huge boundary to cross for me!

What I didn't know at that time, is that The Holy Catholic Church has been in a similar life changing struggle of its own this whole time. It is a struggle that they have yet to reconcile. The struggle they face is between what they are and what they have become. Sometimes after you have built something *so* big and *so* pervasive that turning back would be an unmitigated disaster of epic proportions, you might become too frightened to move; to *do something*! To repent. I do have some empathy for them. I know very well what it feels like to wake up one day and get slapped in the face with the realization that everything you think you know is wrong.

I began to feel lighter as I considered the possibilities. It had never occurred to me before, that my teachers could be wrong. They were my teachers, for heaven's sake! Finally, I heaved a heavy sigh as I decided in that moment to surrender, though the heavens may fall. I vowed to stop lying!

I am Gay! I have always been gay, and I will always be gay.

The war that had always raged in me was *finally* over! I had fed the good wolf. Looking back through the decades since that warm summer day, sitting in that chair with my feet propped up on the window sill, I realize that I have never looked back to wonder if I had made the right decision. There has never been a reason to!

ABOUT THE AUTHOR

G L Franklyn

A native of Detroit, MI, G L Franklyn has lived in Portland, OR since 1987. He is a longtime LGBTQ+ activist and advocate. Along the way, he has had a number of careers, including 3-time award winning Television Producer/Director, A small time Singer/Songwriter in the 80s and, most recently, a Social Worker helping homeless men find and maintain stable housing. He's gay and a hold-over from the Hippy Movement of the 70's. Since 2007 he has been writing in an apparently secret internet blog, spouting off about politics. Today he enjoys a quiet life in a trailer park with his cat, Miss Thing, where he is still trying to figure out what he wants to do with his life.

Made in the USA
Las Vegas, NV
18 June 2023

73553060R00115